Comedy High and Low

Comedy High and Low:

An Introduction
to the Experience of Comedy

MAURICE CHARNEY

PETER LANG
New York · Bern · Frankfurt am Main · Paris

Library of Congress Cataloging-in-Publication Data

Charney, Maurice.
  Comedy high and low.

  Bibliography: p.
  Includes index.
  1. Comedy. 2. Comic, The. I. Title.
  PN1922.C5 1987, 1991, 1993 809.2'523   87-3781
  ISBN 0-8204-0538-8

CIP-Kurztitelaufnahme der Deutschen Bibliothek

Charney, Maurice:
Comedy high and low : an introd. to the ex-
perience of comedy / Maurice Charney. — New
York; Bern; Frankfurt am Main; Paris: Lang,
1987, 1991, 1993
  ISBN 0-8204-0538-8

The paper in this book meets the guidelines for permanence and durability
of the Committee on Production Guidelines for Book Longevity of the
Council on Library Resources.

Originally published 1978 by Oxford University Press

© Peter Lang Publishing, Inc., New York 1987, 1991, 1993, 2005

Printed in the United States of America.

for
my son
LEOPOLD
who knows when to laugh

Preface

My experience in teaching a large undergraduate course in comedy at Rutgers provided the impetus for this book, and especially the difficulty I had in explaining why I thought something was comic. I hadn't realized beforehand how puzzling a subject comedy is. The historical background was no barrier, and the theoretical literature (especially that of Bergson and Freud) lent itself to professorial intervention, but when it came to discussing the reading, I soon discovered that there was no common vocabulary or rhetoric of comedy to draw on. There were no common assumptions and no set of conventions by which we could agree on how to speak about comedy. Others teaching or studying must also have felt this gap or blank in our critical discourse and no doubt in our literary values. For tragedy, Aristotle's *Poetics* offers a reliable guide; despite its extreme brevity, it establishes enough important distinctions and concepts for a whole semester's work. And these ideas about tragedy have really penetrated our general culture. For comedy, however, we have no useful critical tools such as pity and fear, tragic flaw, and catharsis. In fact, among our humanistic values comedy has a very low status indeed, and students feel a certain guilt about taking a course that isn't "serious."

The primary purpose of *Comedy High and Low* is to demonstrate how we can talk about comedy, or, if we cannot arrive at definite conclusions, we can at least try out various kinds of discourse. I would like to be able to answer questions such as: Why is something comic? What conventions is the author drawing on? What traditional patterns of movement are used in any particular work? What assumptions about the nature of comedy does the author make? How does the author evoke laughter, and what purposes does the laughter serve? What are the objects of ridicule, and does the author cover himself by ironic self-deprecation? What comic personae or masks does the author adopt in order to displace and stylize whatever may be too personal in his work? This is just a sampling of questions that need to be answered to help us understand the art of comedy and to encourage us to speak about it.

In general, I have minimized the scholarly, theoretical, and historical backgrounds on which this book is based and attempted to translate and paraphrase ideas into a practical and contemporary form. I would like to be able to bridge the gap between comic literature, especially stage comedy, and the popular comedy of jokes, graffiti, and the grotesque happenings of daily life. It seems to me axiomatic that there is a link between street comedy and the plays of Shakespeare and Molière. This analogy involves assumptions about the relation of literature to experience (and the strength literary language receives from its contact with experience), on one side, and the artfulness of experience on the other. We must believe that high and low comedy fertilize each other, rather than being set apart in antithetical social worlds. Something of what was thought vulgar in Shakespeare by neoclassical critics helps to account for his enormous comic vitality and inventiveness. To complete the circle, I am confident that tellers of jokes benefit from their reading of Aristophanes, Molière, Shakespeare, and other "high" literature.

I have tried to make *Comedy High and Low* a practical book with three large objectives: (1) to consider the popular roots of comedy in jokes, graffiti, riddles, verbal games, nonsense, and other spontaneous, unlearned, folk sources; (2) to offer an account of comedy as a literary art, with examples primarily from stage comedy; (3) to provide students with an introduction to major questions and debates in the theory of comedy (with some attention to unresolved or unresolvable points). These aims may sometimes overlap each other, but I have pursued them together because they are so fundamentally interreiated. The book is arranged as a mosaic of brief topics intended to open a discussion rather than to complete it. I realize that these analytic fragments may tease and perhaps frustrate the reader, but if they also whet the appetite, I feel that my purpose has been served. The slogan-titles are meant to encourage browsing—the reader should be able to dip into the book at any point and encounter a self-contained unit. As a matter of principle, I have tried to be speculative, suggestive, and empirical, and to maintain a receptive and eclectic attitude to the subject.

My examples are drawn mostly from the major figures of stage comedy, because I wanted to concentrate on a single art. There are also many allusions to the great film comedians: Buster Keaton, Charlie Chaplin, W. C. Fields, the Marx Brothers, and their best modern successor, Woody Allen. After much reflection, I decided not to use any examples from the rich literature of comic fiction—Fielding, Smollett, Sterne, Dickens, Lewis Carroll, Heller, Bellow, Salinger, and Pynchon, to name only a few of the many possibilities that come to mind. It seemed to me that the examples from fiction would conflict with those from the theater. Since the two arts of comedy are not really comparable, it would only confuse matters to speak of them together. By virtue of this strong emphasis on drama, *Comedy High and Low* offers an incidental mini-history of stage comedy, with special attention to Shakespeare, Jonson, and Elizabethan drama, Aristophanes, Plautus, Molière, Oscar

Wilde, the drama of the Restoration, and the modern development of tragic farce, particularly in Beckett, Pinter, Dürrenmatt, Ionesco, Orton, and Stoppard.

In a brief preview of the book, I outline six points about the comic experience that represent my underlying assumptions: that comedy is discontinuous, accidental, autonomous, self-conscious, histrionic, and ironic. The reader will undoubtedly discover that I have a penchant for what is usually called "black comedy." This is a temperamental bias, but I have chosen rather to indulge my own intuitions about the meaning of comedy in the late twentieth century—and especially contemporary ideas about comedy as an expression of irrational, unsocialized, chaotic, and wish-fulfillment impulses—than to provide a comprehensive account of the whole history and development of the art.

The book proper begins with the language and rhetoric of comedy, because this represents comedy in its most basic, nonliterary, nonintellectual sense. This is the world of jokes, stories, slogans, graffiti, buttons, and embarrassing situations, chosen to illustrate various modes of comic expression. A variety of histrionic techniques are explored, including creative nonsense and Socratic irony, or the feigning of stupidity for some cunning purpose. The abiding assumption in this chapter is that the comedy of daily life feeds the more elaborate and artful comedy found in literature. There is a continuous line between the language and rhetoric of ordinary, spontaneous, folk comedy and comedy that is meant to be read or performed.

The discussion of comic characters that follows stresses traditions and conventions of character creation, and especially the interplay between stock characters and the comic inventiveness with which they are presented. There is often a wild energy in comic characters that asserts itself despite the conventional limits within which the character is supposed to function. Thus the moral norms are often (and delightfully) violated, although comedies tend to pay lip service to a strict and corrective morality. Comedy is, in essence, a self-generating art, with its own internal history, rather than an art that is produced by ethical assumptions and directives.

We continue with the relatively fixed structures of the comic action, whose beginnings, middles, and ends follow traditional patterns of expectation. The happy ending is achieved regardless of what precedes it. Comic dramatists indulge in intriguing complications for their own sake, since we know how comedies must end. The comedy is a form of display for all kinds of madness, irrationality, and eccentricity, none of which is in any way threatening or dire. Repetition in all of its forms is crucial to the structure—and also the metaphysics—of comedy, since comedy revels in overemphasis and exaggeration. Thus the comic structure becomes an intricate machine, in which ends follow preordained means, but not in any fully predictable manner.

Chapter four is devoted to six representative and interrelated forms of comedy: farce, tragic farce, burlesque, comedy of manners, satire, and festive comedy. I am painfully aware of how many other kinds of comedy, especially pastoral and romantic, I have omitted, but this is only a sampling of a much larger subject. This section leaves comic theory aside and turns to actual plays and playwrights to illustrate the art of comedy. One undeveloped assumption is that all of these six genres bear a type resemblance to farce, which I consider the purest and most absolute form of comedy. Even if the reader doesn't agree with this assumption, it is remarkable how much continuity there is between different kinds of comedy in widely different periods. Both Aristophanes and Dürrenmatt, for example, seem to be addressing themselves to the same petty stupidity, greed, and self-love in their societies.

The final chapter, which postulates seven aspects of the comic hero, draws on the extensive theoretical literature on comedy. I have preferred not to confront this literature directly, since it is often couched in the abstract and technical terminology of philosophy and psychology. Instead, I try out a set of propositions about the comic hero: why he is shown to be invulnerable and omnipotent, indulging in wish fulfillment and fantasy gratification, a player in the literal sense of the term, a realist who celebrates the body, but often also defensive and even paranoid in his approach to reality, a ritual clown and scapegoat. The final postulate is that the comic hero is in a separate world of discourse from the tragic hero, that the two do not tend to merge into each other. These suggestions are offered in a tentative and playful spirit, as possibilities rather than as facts, and readers are encouraged to argue back and to draw their own conclusions.

The book concludes with a chapter-by-chapter account of

sources, with suggestions for further reading. I hope that this will offer some directions for finding one's way in the vast literature on the subject. My secret wish is that *Comedy High and Low: An Introduction to the Experience of Comedy* will stimulate readers to have their own comic experience and to read and think further about this puzzling art.

For my intellectual sources in writing this book, I owe an enormous debt to Henri Bergson's *Laughter (Le Rire)*, published in 1900, which relies heavily on farce and social comedy, especially that of Molière. I have borrowed from Bergson continually, but without specifically mentioning it, since my obligation to him is so obvious. I am also constantly arguing with Sigmund Freud's theories of comedy, as presented chiefly in *Jokes and Their Relation to the Unconscious (Der Witz und seine Beziehung zum Unbewussten)*, published in 1905, because Freud is so enormously fertile, imaginative, and stimulating in his interpretations—infuriating, too, but Freud never lacked the energy of his commitments. Bergson and Freud are the two most important influences on this book. I have also drawn significantly on the theories of Francis Cornford and Northrop Frye about Plautus and New Comedy, the ideas of Cedric Whitman on Aristophanes and Old Comedy, and Mikhail Bakhtin and C. L. Barber on festive comedy.

I have read widely in the specialized studies of comedy by psychologists and psychoanalysts. Their attempts to be scientific, however, are sometimes unintentionally droll. It is surely helpful to know the favorite jokes of suicidal patients, and there is a whole minor literature of the favorite joke as a diagnostic tool. When we read Ludwig Eidelberg's minute analysis of a joke by Mae West—(1) Mae West returns home and finds ten sailors in her bedroom. She says: (2) I am tired; (3) two must go—we are not sure whether this is a burlesque in its own right or a formal study of the psychodynamics of jokes. It is certainly both at the same time, as is Frederic Stearns's account of a laughing epidemic in Tanganyika and Uganda between January 1962 and June 1964 that affected about 1000 persons, mostly young adolescent girls from Catholic convent schools. Stearns is fascinated by the deeply infectious and almost incurable nature of this epidemic. Perhaps a vaccination will be discovered that will protect innocent persons from the sudden ravages of uncontrollable laughter.

In the midst of Eric Bentley's vigorous apology for farce in *The Life of the Drama*, I was surprised to find the following remarks on laughter: "That what purport to be studies of comedy often turn out to be only studies of laughter is to be regretted, yet the circumstance faithfully reflects the mentality of the comedian." I feel rather shamefaced about quoting this, since my book is mainly concerned with laughing comedy (or comedy that makes you laugh) and tends to neglect moral and socially corrective comedy, as well as comedy in the largest sense of Dante's *Divine Comedy* or Homer's *Odyssey*. When I speak of laughter, I am not thinking of that superbly ironic laughter of the gods that Homer mentions, but rather of the more mundane laughter that accompanies jokes, the routines of clowns and stand-up comedians, and the witty dialogue and characterizations of stage comedy. To provoke the *fou rire*, as the French call an involuntary, furious, and prolonged fit of laughter, is one of the great accomplishments of comedy. I hope Bentley will forgive me, as a critic of comedy, for claiming "the circumstance [that] faithfully reflects the mentality of the comedian." If we can agree on that point, his quotation, as they say in the classics, will not be a total loss.

I am indebted to the many persons who had the patience to tell me jokes (especially Don Wiener, Alvin Lukashok, and David Gordon), or whose jokes I overheard in the subway, in telephone booths, in coffee shops, and on interstate buses (especially the glabrous and agelastic Suburban Transit) and trains (of the aptly named Conrail System), and whose graffiti I read with avid curiosity. I have expropriated and refashioned all of these jokes and inscriptions with the full license and anonymity that is usually attributed to the collective folk unconscious. I am grateful to many students at Rutgers—they know who they are—who helped me overcome my timidity and who patiently explained to me the meaning of words like "funky," "foxy," and "the pits," in courses in farce, theory of comedy, drama of the sixties, and literature and sexuality.

I owe special thanks to Steve Helmling, who asked me to speak on comedy to the English Graduate Club at Rutgers; to Dick Brucher, who invited me to read a chapter of this book at the University of Maine; and to Tom Clayton, who offered the splendid facilities of the University of Minnesota as a forum for my speculations on comedy. I want to applaud all those bold persons who asked questions and made vociferous and well-phrased objections. Peter Caws helped me to define my subject (or at least to curb my over-ripe fancy) and Jeanine Plottel fed me with bibliographical references (especially to the more arcane psychoanalytic literature), as if they were the stuff of life. Margaret Ganz had the kindness to send me a set of her offprints on comedy and to explain what they really meant. Terry Hawkes provided me with authoritative information on tag lines and British colloquial, along with the characteristic gestures that accompany them; it is a pity that these cannot be included in this volume. John Richetti offered an exceptionally full and bibliographical answer (with appropriate refreshments) to a question on Samuel Johnson. At a critical moment, Mary Ann Caws proffered a typewriter. My wife Hanna found no aspect of this book too trivial to discuss, and she reminded me, from her own endless stock of continental erudition, of all the good things I was omitting (and some of which I afterwards included). The Wertheim Study of the New York Public Library gave me an excellent retreat to read the literature on comedy without being apprehended for disturbing the peace. I am grateful, finally, to the Research Council of Rutgers University and to its distinguished Maecenas, Fred Main, for financing a semester off during which this project was begun.

For the illustrations, I wish to thank Mary Corliss of the Museum of Modern Art/Film Stills Archives for patiently introducing me to rich materials previously unknown to me. Paula Klaw of Movie Star News also made many suggestions about ways to furrow in her vast collection of stills. Figures 5, 7, 9–15, 19, and 20 are from the Museum of Modern Art; the frontispiece and Figures 17 and 18 are from Movie Star News. For Figure 2 the Metropolitan Museum of Art supplied a photograph of a print in its collections. I am grateful to the following publishers for permission to reproduce copyrighted material: *The New Yorker* for the Handelsman cartoon (Figure 6), Dial Press for the Glashan cartoon (Figure 1), and *Private Eye* for the cartoon "Social Scene" (Figure 16).

Contents

Comedy High and Low

Preview

The comic experience is such a vast subject that it is difficult to generalize about it. But, more importantly, comedy may not be a single, identifiable subject, for which any individual theory or set of data will be adequate. The Superiority Theory lends itself to certain kinds of aggressive jokes, Bergson's ideas about the mechanization of the life-force applies best to farce (where characterization is limited), Freud's conception of wit and the unconscious works beautifully for dirty jokes or comedy in which forbidden impulses are expressed, anthropological theories fit various forms of aris-

3

tophanic Old Comedy in which there is a scapegoat and a ritual hero, and other principles and ideas about comedy all have their special cases to which they apply most aptly, but there is also a whole other literature to which they don't apply at all. Throughout the book I assume that there cannot, in the nature of things, be a unified theory of comedy relevant to the whole range of comic experience. I have therefore tried to follow, without excessive apology, my own predilection for irony and black comedy.

The emphasis is on comedy that makes you laugh, and there is an underlying connection between the popular comedy of jokes and the more formal comedy of plays and literature. Movies represent a middle ground between literature and the oral tradition. Although examples are drawn from a wide range of sources, I have assumed that these sources have something in common. Thus, various mechanisms of jokes—surprise, incongruity, acceleration of climax, sudden deflation of expectations—may also operate in the more literate world of stage comedy. Laughter, in some tangible, physiological sense, validates the comic experience and offers a common denominator between jokes and literature. Not that there cannot be a great deal of excellent comedy without laughter; we don't need actual, explosive laughter that can be measured on a laughometer. We can also smile quietly at what we consider droll, but comedy demands a strong reaction, however it is expressed externally.

Freud made an important link between jokes and dreams, and his book on jokes was the outgrowth of his book on dreams. This is a vital connection. Comedy may be anchored in ordinary, daily experience—what is usually lumped together under the concerns of realism—but the comic effects depend upon forays into the unexplored territory of wish fulfillment and fantasy gratification. "Fantasy" is an inaccurate psychological word for what literary critics would call the imagination. This is the area where dreams and comedy work together to realize a broad gamut of human potentialities. Dreams and jokes release imaginative materials that would otherwise remain buried in the unconscious. Since tragedy focusses so strongly on psychological truth, it has a natural affinity for realism and naturalism, or at least for some accurate and ethical account of how ordinary experience impinges on the nature of things.

At its best, comedy offers us a mode of perception. We may use our comic intuition to display and master our own anxious demons, or to express freely and with abandon our regressive and infantile impulses, as in John Glashan's wonderfully irresponsible cartoon from *Speak Up You Tiny Fool* (see Figure 1). The vastness of the audience and the portentousness of the occasion are essential for defining the orator's comic inadequacy. We also need comedy for its metaphysical and stylistic possibilities: comedy has a close connection with lifestyle. In this larger sense, it provides a form of awareness by which we may understand and deal with a puzzling reality. Our best contemporary writers of comedy—Beckett, Pinter, Dürrenmatt, Ionesco, Orton, Stoppard—all use comic intuition to structure the world of their plays. They make assumptions about the fallibility of reason, the difficulty of communication, and the preposterousness of language that support a concept of black comedy.

We may pursue a metaphysics of comedy in six distinct areas, which may conveniently define the comic experience. Briefly stated, comedy is discontinuous, accidental, autonomous, self-conscious, histrionic, and ironic. Most of these are overlapping and mutually defining terms, but we may deal with them in separate categories. By way of preview, we may make some minimal observations about these six areas and their relation to the art of comedy:

> *1. The Discontinuous:* Comedy depends on the breaking of rational order and causality. We may abruptly shift perspective and juxtapose separate pieces of action as if they belonged with each other. The time sequence is flexible and subject-object relations may be reversed. The overall feeling is one of uneasiness, since the patterns created are crazyquilts and random mosaics.
>
> *2. The Accidental:* We need to have faith in the validity and significance of random experience, the fortuitous and the unanticipated. This posits a grand creativity in nature, so that any event, no matter how trivial, may have rich comic possibilities: a walk down the street, browsing among unrelated books, a visit to the town dump. What happens

Figure 1. Comedy as a Vehicle for Expressing and Mastering Anxiety (John Glashan, *Speak Up You Tiny Fool*, New York: The Dial Press, 1966, copyright © 1961, 1966 by John Glashan; *reprinted by permission of the publisher*).

spontaneously happens rightly and therefore feeds the comic imagination.

3. The Autonomous: Things have a life of their own. The distinction between the organic and inorganic worlds is false. Material things can be animated if observed closely enough. Machines suggest comic analogies between the life of things and the life of man. Things can be recombined into new and meaningful relations that comment on each other. Clowns have always tried to imitate the inanimate world.

4. The Self-Conscious: The body is a material object, and the intense and minute awareness of the body is a vital source of comedy. The separable parts of the body support the mechanical analogy and raise anxieties about castration, impotence, and loss of mechanical function. To be a human being is inherently comic. Can we be reconciled to our own organic disgust?

5. The Histrionic: Man is an actor playing a clownish role. We are intensely aware of the meaninglessness of our attempts to communicate. Language is a fallible instrument and words float freely in a magic reality. The enormous sea of words represents possibilities of expression that can never be used. Words are gestural and have a life of their own available for comic exploitation. Once words and actions are separated from communicable meaning, they are freed of their utilitarian taint. The clown engages more often in soliloquy than in conversation.

6. The Ironic: We are forced back to the basic assumption of dreams and poetry: that everything can also mean its opposite. Comedy trains us to expect the pie in the face. Language is especially rife with ironic possibilities, since this is the medium of rational discourse. The ironist is a sly man who is constantly repeating: the only thing I know is that I know nothing. This kind of openness makes a good beginning for comedy.

I

The Language and Rhetoric of Comedy

To begin with the most basic skills, there is a language and a rhetoric of comedy as well established and as practical in its assumptions as the language and rhetoric of public speaking. Comedy, too, is an art of persuasion, that tries to move its auditors to laughter, which is the proper end of comedy. Perhaps we should say laughter or its equivalent, since we need not laugh out loud to express our delight. In the most extreme case, Lord Chesterfield advised his son that "there is nothing so illiberal and so ill-bred as audible laughter" (Letter of March 9, 1748). To generate laughter places a heavy burden on comedy—we could not demand that tragedy move us to tears—a pragmatic and almost measurable burden.

What makes comedy effective? This chapter is devoted to verbal devices and abilities that have been traditionally associated with comedy, but we should also take account of the vast resources of nonverbal humor. The great age of comedy in the American silent films was entirely without words, if one discounts the captions, which may have been useful for narrative, but did nothing for the comedy. Joke-telling is an oral art, and there is nothing paler than an anthology of printed jokes. The classic *Joe Miller's Jests: or, The Wits Vade-Mecum* (1739) seems only a literary curiosity now that it has lost its connection with performance. Like musical scores, books of jokes are only the notation for something that needs to be realized in another medium. And the effect of great clowns and comedians can only be dimly recounted to those who have not heard them. Like acting itself, comedy is immediate and momentary. Its success is unpredictable, even from joke to joke or from one performance to another. Despite the traditional art, training, and practice required of actors and comedians, there remains a spontaneous energy and a surprising effect that cannot properly be anticipated or taken for granted.

Irony lies at the heart of comic technique. All comedy is a manipulation of deceptive appearances.

The most triumphantly ironic act is to pretend to be stupid. This is the function of the *eiron*, a character much favored in the criticism of Francis Cornford and Northrop Frye, and a figure out of the characterology of Aristotle's *Poetics*. He is the original ironist: the sly, subtle, deceptive, wily man who tries to confuse you. The *eiron* keeps telling us that things are not what they seem, that reality is an illusion, and that appearances may be different from the truth. He is a manipulator because reality itself is shifting and unstable. Objective facts and the evidence of our senses are not to be trusted; we must poke around for ourselves and remain skeptical, open, and loose. If nothing is dependable and solid, then reality may be a projection of our own wayward thoughts, and we are back at the wish-fulfillment images of comedy. Once we admit there are blanks, then we also have to agree that we may fill them as we choose.

Socrates is the great *eiron* of antiquity. He plays the fool, feigns ignorance, asks seemingly innocent and childlike questions that are meant to trap you. Socratic irony is still usually defined as a pretended stupidity, a disingenuousness and false naivety intended to mislead its hearers and to produce a result strikingly different from what they counted on. What could be more infuriating than Socrates' continual assertion: "The only thing I know is that I know nothing"? Socrates' confidential manner and his disarming questions suggest that, like the tricky slave of Roman comedy, he has deliberately adopted a comic persona: he is the comic philosopher *par excellence*. He is uncouth, a notable drinker (as in the *Symposium*), convivial, hearty, bluff, candid, and a man driven out of his home by a shrewish wife, Xantippe. All of these qualities generate an enormous admiration and sympathy for him, yet he is also playing a public role, for which he creates a public personality. By his wit, he seeks to banish falsehood and pretense and to discover what all men need to know in order to lead the good life. The *eiron* may be an entertainer and even a wise guy in some of his aspects, but Socrates was also a sacred fool, dedicated to the truth at the risk of his own life. He is our first great comic martyr.

Irony is more a mood than a metaphysical assumption in comedy, and it may account for the unusual alertness demanded of the comic hero. He must, at all costs, be ready for whatever turns up, and not only ready, but also skillful, versatile, ingenious, spontaneous, and improvisatory. He must seem to perform miracles with only the slightest of materials. That is why magic is a frequent metaphor for comedy, as if the comedian could actually produce illusions. He is a magician only in his ability to manipulate chance and to conjure up desired situations. Even juggling is subject to gravity; however, the art of juggling is organized not to defy gravity but to ignore it—remember that W. C. Fields began his career as a juggler. So the ironic comedian makes everything look easy. He is always graceful, aristocratic, casual, and tremendously natural. The ultimate art is to annihilate all traces of art, all artfulness or effort. The ironic comedian practices the law of the conservation of energy.

Irony is more a lifestyle than a specific comic technique, and nowhere is irony more prevalent than in Jewish humor. If this is a defensive, ghetto humor where nothing can be assumed and in which the future is a vaguely threatening possibility, then one can understand the dominance of the interrogative mode. A question is always answered with a question in order to dignify the original question and to shore up a questionable reality, as in the familiar exchange: A: "Why do Jews answer a question with a question?" B: "Why shouldn't Jews answer a question with a question?"

A boy of thirteen going to a new barber asked with fear and trembling, "How much does a haircut cost?" The barber being Jewish and not Italian (which was the proper ethnic association for barbers) ignored the question and said only, "Why don't you sit down and take it easy?" Once in the chair (the Chair!), the boy managed to ask again, feebly, "How much does a haircut cost?" This time the barber, already tightening the cloth around the boy's neck, addressed himself to the question with an overwhelming counter-question, "How much can a haircut cost?" With characteristic slyness and aplomb, the barber refused to grapple directly with stupidity and a notable loss of perspective. Jewish irony pits the powerless little man, who may, for all one knows, be a schlemiel or a nebbish, against an all-powerful world, in which he is expected to bluff his way to victory. Anything is possible. It is all a matter of saying the right word or pulling the right card out of your sleeve.

Irony may be a survival technique, but it is comic because of the gross disproportion between subject and object. There is no corresponding magnitude, weight, or gravity, and it looks as if the ironic fool will, through a cunning display of meekness, inherit the earth. Winner take all, but how can you cope with a winner who looks like a loser? The confusion is deliberate. The ironic fool is a master of disguise, who cultivates illusions and false appearances. Wariness is all: be on your guard, don't let your defenses down—and there seems to be an automatic assumption that life is a struggle between ill-matched forces, in which the weakest always wins.

The ironic style may be conscious or unconscious, but the effects are the same. In other words, if an ironist engages in self-parody, it is done out of cunning mockery, but if a blunt and foolish person speaks in a style that is hopelessly banal, the result may be similar despite the fact that the motives are strikingly different.

Parody usually involves either the words and syntax of some authentic original, or else a feeling that some potential original is being skillfully violated. Thus, Oliver Jensen's parody of the Gettysburg Address in Eisenhowerese is a takeoff on the dismal, bureaucratic jargon of the Eisenhower era, in which the flatness, dullness, and colorlessness of its meandering style function like an overpowering anesthetic:

> I haven't checked these figures but 87 years ago, I think it was, a number of individuals organized a governmental set-up here in this country, I believe it covered certain Eastern areas, with this idea they were following up based on a sort of national independence arrangement and the program that every individual is just as good as every other individual. Well, now, of course, we are dealing with this big difference of opinion, civil disturbance you might say, although I don't like to appear to take sides or name any individuals, and the point is naturally to check up, by actual experience in the field. . . .

The parody continues with endless proliferation.

If we turn now to President Eisenhower's West Point Address of June 5, 1960, the parody is immediately put to shame as a bungling, amateur attempt to imitate the authentic original:

> But we wonder what is the outcome of every decent, proper gesture we make to those that live in the other camp. They live in a closed society, secrecy of intent—which we try to penetrate, and in my opinion properly, but we are certain of this: Our problem is not only keeping ourselves strong, and by strong I don't mean merely militarily, I mean spiritually, intellectually, scientifically, economically and militarily; and then, we

Figure 2. Caricature: Louis Philippe Being Transformed into a
Poire ("Pear" and "Fathead") by Charles Philipon in *Charivari*,
January 17, 1834 (*The Metropolitan Museum of Art, Gift of Arthur Sachs, 1923*).

must make certain that all of those people who live with us, in the hope that those concepts of human dignity and freedom and liberty are going to prevail in the world, will stand always by our side in the determination that freedom and liberty will eventually triumph over tyranny. . . .

Which is the real parody? I don't think we need to prove intent to convict President Eisenhower of self-parody. He takes liberties with himself that Oliver Jensen doesn't dare to assume, and we get lost in a tundra of vast meaninglessness. There is a perverse brilliance in President Eisenhower's uncompleted parentheses within parentheses, winding syntax, lost clauses, and textbook anacolutha.

Parody always involves an element of stylistic caricature: we are so characteristically like ourselves that we automatically become absurd. Caricature is a term from the fine arts, especially drawing, in which one easily recognizable feature of a person is exaggerated, so that the person is ridiculed. The subject may be given a swinish, unctuous, sensual, or otherwise dishonest air, and only the single, emphasized trait has any significance. Caricature is a form of grotesque vilification, as in Charles Philipon's powerful cartoon of 1834 showing Louis Philippe, the "Citizen King" of France (1830–1848), in the act of becoming a *poire* (both "pear" and "fathead" in French—see Figure 2).

Burlesque is a gentler term than caricature, used chiefly for literary examples, to indicate a damaging takeoff on one's work or manner. In a pastiche, a number of different styles may be pieced together to make an amusing farrago or medley of unrelated items. This is parody of the most virtuoso sort. Another kind of parody is the mock-encomium or mock-panegyric, in which one pretends to praise something one loathes; it is damning with faint praise. In the mock-heroic, the epic style is imitated for a ridiculous subject or situation, and the humor arises from the gross disproportion between the elevated style and the base materials.

All of these examples draw an ironic contrast between matter and manner, subject and object, style and purpose, and the humor arises from the skill of the writer in malicious imitation of some real or imagined original. The parodist understands the art of bathos,

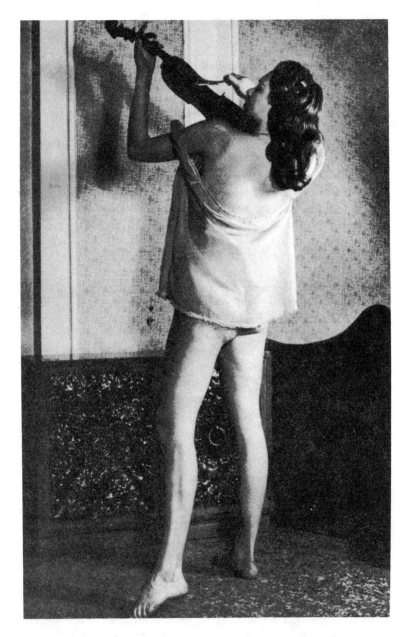

Figure 3. Pornokitsch: A Lightly Clad Violinist in a Pseudo-Elegant Setting (from Gillo Dorfles, *Kitsch: The World of Bad Taste*, New York: Universe Books, 1969).

Figure 4. Pornokitsch: A Crudely Idealized Nude Violinist in a
Romantic Setting (from Gillo Dorfles, *Kitsch: The World of Bad Taste*, New York:
Universe Books, 1969).

or sudden sinkings and precipitous descents in formal usage. Comparisons between the high and the low, the grand and the base, the noble and the infamous may not only be odious, but also bathetic, if accomplished with appropriate swiftness, incoherence, and lack of transition. The false sentiment of bathos is meant to be contrasted with the authentic passion of pathos.

The final resting-place of irony is in that ill-defined junk heap of the imagination vaguely characterized as camp or kitsch. Transvestites are camp, and so are 1930s musicals (especially the costumes), tap dancing, hooked rugs, crewel garters, hand-worked samplers, cranked phonographs with cactus needles that need to be sharpened, glass shoes, sequined dresses, roses of all sorts (especially artificial ones, and, more especially, silk ones with beads), mandolin music, the use of the subjunctive, steamer trunks, and everything distantly related to the experience of going to camp—a time when one is unusually responsive to sentimentality. And what about old autograph albums? All of this third-rate paraphernalia, sometimes termed "junque" in the trade, is encrusted with an emotional significance and a tenderness that is consciously false. The nostalgic mood is crawling with self-parody, and yet there is a sickly authenticity of lost youth clinging about the enterprise.

Kitsch is the Teutonic equivalent of bad art, which has important cultural differences from the strictly American camp. Nude violinists or ladies in full dress with riding crops are not exactly the American idea of fun, yet kitsch and camp can be matched item for item on a parallel list. Kitsch has a natural aspiration to pornokitsch, in which very real and strikingly uncomfortable and gauche naked women are frozen in idealized settings, as in the portraits of violinists in Figures 3 and 4. The viewer is puzzled about how to interpret these pseudo-aesthetic pictures. One's confidence is immediately shaken by the fact that the model in the painting is holding the violin with the wrong arm. The mood of slightly soiled innocence and factory seconds of real experience permeates the concept of kitsch and camp, which offers a tawdry comic escape to overly sophisticated persons. Camp and kitsch are a modern parody of pastoral innocence and naivety, expressed in a bucolic setting with (or without) sheep, shepherdesses, and camp counselors.

Language is a vast sea of comic possibilities swirling beneath rational discourse.

Current theories of language emphasize the expressive capabilities of words, because the sign functions are quickly exhausted. Language is play, we talk for amusement, and one of the most primitive purposes of communication may have been to tell jokes rather than to locate a reliable food supply or pliable mates. In current primitive societies, the sense of humor is often highly developed. For one thing their culture is primarily oral. Writing, and especially printing (as Marshall McLuhan has so powerfully demonstrated in *The Gutenberg Galaxy*), tends to fix and stabilize meanings which might otherwise remain open and fluid. In an oral culture, the sounds are literally the basic units of meaning, with almost unlimited possibilities for punning. The awareness of spelling tends to restrict the free play of the comic imagination.

We know that Shakespeare's spelling was much less rigid than ours and that he spelled his name differently in the same document. Phonetically, some of Shakespeare's characters are revealingly characterized. Thus the melancholy Jaques takes his name from "jakes," the new-fangled word for a privy; Pistol is "pizzle," the penis of an animal, usually a bull; and Bolingbroke, spelled Bullingbrooke in the Folio, is associated with the "bull" of the first syllable of his apt name. Or what about the potential wordplay postulated between Falstaff ("Fall staff") and Shakespeare ("Shake spear")? Once we insist on the sound of words as the basic verbal reality of a play (and the spelling as only something secondary and arbitrary), these sounds set off resemblances and relationships in our mind. Thus the neutral word "madam" contains the sound-unit "mad," and it may conceivably stimulate an anagrammatic relation with "madman" and even "madonna"—all "mad" words and relevant to the dialogue of Olivia and her fool Feste in *Twelfth Night* (Act I, Scene v).

Many limericks depend upon oral puns, as in the much-quoted lines of Langford Reed:

An indolent vicar of Bray
His roses allowed to decay.
His wife, more alert,
Bought a powerful squirt
And said to her spouse, "Let us spray."

This is not a subtle example—limericks are rarely subtle—but the spoken words must be the final criterion of wit. There is pleasure in phonetic free association not unlike the joys of daydreaming, as we skip aimlessly from "spray" to "pray" to "prey" to the donkey's "bray" and possibly to the "break" connected with "squirt."

Double entendres, some planned but most fortuitous, lurk everywhere in the English language, whose loss of declensions, conjugations, and exact syntax makes it vulnerable to sexual ambiguity. Any unsecured use of "it" in English is almost automatically sexual, and a vague "do" has similar connotations, as in the request associated with barbers, "May I do you now, sir?", or the suggestive Clairol hair-coloring ads: "Does she or doesn't she? Only her hairdresser knows for sure." Certain words like "fix" have such a multiplicity of meanings that they tend to spark off sexual suggestions unless they are specifically excluded by the context. In speech, of course, even innocent words like "come" and "put" can be instantly endowed with double entendre by a mere gesture or intonation (not to speak of a knowing leer). This gives the English language a quality of phonetic innuendo that may not be present in other, more exactly inflected language systems.

Verbal games, riddles, puzzles, and conundrums are usually based on puns or outrageous wordplay—outrageous because they deal us such a stunning phonetic blow that we recoil at our own infantile amusement. These kinds of jokes, so appealing to children, fulfill Hobbes's definition of laughter as a "sudden glory." The question-answer form of conundrums is particularly satisfying to the young, because it offers the chance to assert their superiority over dull-witted adults, who cannot answer the question. Again, this kind of humor supports the Hobbesian theory of laughter as the expression of superiority—not just mental superiority, but an almost physical domination by the powerful aggressor over his helpless prey. On *Can You Top This?*, a radio program of the 1940s, a panel of distinguished joke-tellers tried to outdo each other's jokes, and the laughter of the audience was scientifically measured on a "laughometer." This competitiveness of jokes seems to be an entirely natural phenomenon. Joke-tellers are usually compulsively neurotic, and they don't stop until they have decisively defeated every other joke-teller in the room. Perhaps expressions like "This one will knock you dead," or "This one will kill you," come out of a need for dominance, in which the joke-teller must assert his magical powers over his passive auditors.

Besides one's immediate family, one of the best sources for riddles and conundrums is Darwin A. Hindman's *1800 Riddles, Enigmas and Conundrums*. Hindman has a special section of biblical conundrums, all smacking of Sunday school and church picnics. "Why was there no card-playing on Noah's Ark? Because Noah sat on the deck." "Where were the children of Israel when the lights went out? In the dark." Try this highly sophisticated riddle, unanswerable by mere reasoning power: "Why were Pharaoh's daughters the first financiers? Because they took a little prophet [Moses] from the rushes on the bank." We wince at the apt completeness of the answer. It is superfluous to say that the joke turns on a trick question that is not a question at all, but we feel stymied by our inability to answer, and our feeling of involuntary nonparticipation may account for the rabid hostility some adults show to riddles.

Sometimes the questions go in series, with an ascending (and possibly off-color) climax. "What has four wheels and flies? A garbage truck." "But what has four legs and flies? Two pairs of pants." "But what has sixteen legs, fourteen testicles, and two tiny breasts? Snow White and the Seven Dwarfs." I omit a few of the intervening steps to spare the reader the full unfolding of the numerical progression, but it's obvious that this kind of riddling is part of a primitive contest of wits. In the usual movement, the riddles get stronger and more absurd as the contest warms up. Thus, a child might ask: "What has four hundred legs, six blue eggs, and a machine gun? Four centipedes guarding a robin's nest with a machine gun."

A subspecialty of question-answer jokes are those in which the answer is given first and then the auditor is asked to supply the question. These are generally so farfetched that the listener is astounded (or infuriated) by their ingenuity—usually termed "stupidity" by real aficionados of the art. For example, of what question is the following the answer: "9W"? Admittedly, this is rather arcane, and the fact that 9W was the highway most people took to get up to the Catskills (or Borscht Belt) is merely a red herring. The question, of course, is the one put by the TV interviewer: "Is that Richard Wagner with a 'V'?" ("9W," the answer, translates the German or Yiddish "nein" for "no," with "W" pronounced as "V".) A simpler, or at least a less esoteric example of the art is the following answer: "Washington Irving," which is the logical reply to the question: "Who was the first president of the United States, Max?"

A parallel art is to tell jokes backwards, beginning with the punch line and working one's way forward, as in the following hypothetical and numbered example:

> *1.* One nun says to the other: "Doesn't that gentleman speak beautiful Latin?"
>
> *2.* "Marcus fuctus!" (a stinging exclamation uttered by Max to Irving, or vice versa).
>
> *3.* Max (or Irving) discovers that the suit he has just bought from his brother-in-law Marcus is not black but navy blue. He discovers this by comparing his newly purchased suit with the genuinely black habit of the nuns.
>
> *4.* Max (or Irving) must have a black suit for a formal occasion and goes to his brother-in-law Marcus to buy it. He is assured that the suit is authentically black and not navy blue.

It is apparent that this story is radically improved by telling it in reverse.

These language games are a form of linguistic, phonetic, and logic play. They demonstrate, at least to children, that language is not a monolithic, denotative, rational system invented by adults to dominate the young, but rather a wild, chaotic, irrational, hopelessly funny pot of sounds that can be recombined and regrouped to produce unanticipated meanings. Children delight in finding dirty words concealed in normal words, and since they reason phonetically, they would have no trouble understanding Hamlet's sharp question to Ophelia, "Do you think I meant country matters?" (3.2.119).

Some of the items in Hindman's book are remarkably complicated, but I don't think they are beyond the capacity of a child, which we tend to regularly underestimate. Freud's bald assertion that children have no sense of humor is preposterous (and insulting, too). Martha Wolfenstein has much more respect than Freud for the humor of children in her fine book, *Children's Humor: A Psychological Analysis* (1954), but I can't agree that young children don't engage in elaborate puns and wordplay. The problem may be that psychological researchers forget how overwhelmingly phonetic (rather than written) words are in a child's mind. That's the only way of comprehending this very advanced conundrum in Hindman: "Why is a mahout, when trampled by his elephant, like a lobster? Because he's a crushed Asian [crustacean]."

Off-color riddles work best when the second meaning is not at all obvious, and children love to spring these on you and make you blush, or at least cause some officially acknowledged embarrassment. There is a whole class of conundrums based on transposed sounds, or, more literally, transposed initial letters of words. "What is the difference between someone who has seen Niagara Falls and someone who hasn't? One has seen the mist, the other has missed the scene." This is entirely innocent, but the following is not: "What is the difference between a circus and a burlesque show? One is a cunning array of stunts. . . ." In the same tawdry spirit: "What is the difference between a lady in church and a lady in the bathtub? One has hope in her soul. . . ." These are like naughty limericks, which are meant to demonstrate that language is deceptive, wily, unpredictable, and may play tricks on you. In short, it is inherently ironic.

Strict phonologists (like Helge Kökeritz in *Shakespeare's Pronunciation*) insist that puns must be homophonic, or identical in sound, like sole/soul, cruel/crewel, dual/duel, checks/Czechs, etc., and they are happiest with the same word used in entirely different senses, like the "bill" of a store and the "bill" of a bird—how about a taxidermist's bill? But to limit puns to homophones ignores the vast area of wordplay where the sound-matching is only partial and the punning intent is very apparent, as in queen/quean (especially Shakespeare's Cleopatra), fool/fuel, crux/crooks, violence/violins, beings/beans (as in the exchange, "What kind of beans do cannibals eat? Human beings.").

Perhaps half-puns and quarter-puns, like partial rhymes, make more teasing and poignant examples than the more obvious, full-blooded puns. There are so many brilliant possibilities in the poems of Ogden Nash that it is anticlimactic to quote anything, but I choose the concluding couplet of "Golly, How Truth Will Out!":

> *And that is why I admire a suave prevarication because I*
> *   prevaricate so awkwardly and gauchely,*
> *And that is why I can never amount to anything politically*
> *   or socially.*

We are expected to wince at this seemingly awkward pun/rhyme, which is not awkward at all but a deft corner shot. Ogden Nash (and Dorothy Parker, too) understood the athletic grace of distant, miscegenated rhymes.

A slight deflection of speech may produce puns that were never intended (like Manufacturers Truss Company), which are all the more welcome for constituting a secret language. Many of the terms connected with automotive repair have vaguely punning and sexual overtones, perhaps because the car as a cultural symbol is so heavily anthropomorphized. What are we to make of a ring job, new gaskets, a leak in the exhaust manifold, tappets that don't open, a twisted drive shaft, and indequate torque, not to speak of male and female threads, nipples, sockets, and miscellaneous bushings? Perhaps we need the concept of double entendre to prove the existence of almost continuous, unrelieved, and uninterrupted wordplay in daily life. One of the most charming examples is the gross pun delivered with a full measure of earnestness and sincerity by a French-Canadian mayor of Nashua, New Hampshire, in acknowledgment of applause: "I thank you for the claps you give me and me wife."

Nonsense, both calculated and spontaneous, is one of the chief by-products of language.

If language is a logical and rational system of communication, there is special delight in confuting the system, in affronting it by arrant nonsense that has the ring of significant (if not also poetic and philosophical) expression. This is one of the cornerstones of the attack on the cozy and comfortable assurances of middle-class rationality which was made by writers, painters, and aesthetic exhibitionists associated with Dada and Surrealism. If Tristan Tzara can cut up a poem, put the pieces into a top hat (as in Stoppard's exhilarating play, *Travesties*), and then offer newly fortuitous poems that are better than the originals because they are more spontaneous, then literary texts are no longer to be regarded as fixed and immutable entities. If the words are alive, the literature is available for new combinations; but this may only be a ponderous rationale for aesthetic play.

On the simplest level of non sequiturs, verbal nonsense possesses an air of mystery and unexplored metaphoric potentiality. The displaced logic teases the imagination to complete propositions that cannot logically be completed. We search for the hidden link in the following conditional utterance: "If I had a sister, I'm sure she would love Camembert." The speaker, obviously incestuous in his fantasy, wants to support his own guilty fondness for Camembert with a familial sanction. The following German proverb is familial and domestic in its imaginative thrust: "If my grandmother had wheels, she would be a bus" ("Wenn meine Grossmutter Räder hätt, wär sie ein Autobus"). It is difficult to answer these intrusive postulations except with a reductive and unsatisfying statement of fact: "As luck would have it, my grandmother died before I was born, and I'm sure that my sister—if I ever have one—would prefer Brie." Non sequiturs have the fascination of Cretan Linear B, Irish ogam, and other hieroglyphic alphabets that have not yet been satisfactorily deciphered. By the very nature of our commitment to poetic language, we are forced to believe in their esoteric meaning.

What are we to make of the following statement: "I know an old man in New Zealand who hasn't a tooth in his head, but he can play a bass drum better than any man I ever heard"? Some puzzling link between teeth and drum-playing is hypothecated, and the fact that New Zealand is more than 6,000 miles from New York seems to introduce a new, topographical factor that complicates the original proposition with hints of alienation. We would like to believe that we understand the logic of this statement, just as audiences that listen to double-talk usually take an inordinately long time to figure out that they are hearing a non-language. We are hopelessly vulnerable in our inherent and automatic manufacture—nay secretion—of significance. The humor arises from the frustration of an insatiable need.

Logical nonsense takes the form of pseudo-profundity; the auditor is made to feel that he has missed something important or that he cannot fathom profoundly simple, Zen-like paradoxes because he lacks the poetic sensibility. There is a series of fallacies of daily life—actually, parodies of common sense—that take this form. We may group these under the general heading *The Fallacy of the One-Legged Runner*, which assumes that, contrary to the dull perceptions of common sense, the one-legged runner has a natural superiority to the two-legged runner. This seems to be a takeoff on Aesop's fable of the tortoise and the hare. *The It-Could-Have-Been-Worse Fallacy* is associated with Jewish humor, since it seeks to make the best of a bad situation by imagining worse situations. Thus, if you fall off a ladder and break your arm, you are exceedingly lucky because you might have broken your neck. The joke about the two ties follows the pattern of *The Tainted Alternative:* A mother gives her son two beautiful ties for his birthday; thinking to please his mother, he wears one on Mother's Day, but the mother is obviously chagrined and asks: "What's the matter? You don't like the other one?" The related *Fallacy of the Superior Alternative* asserts that no matter what you finally decide to do, the alternative that you rejected would have been better. Thus, if you serve fish and someone chokes on a bone, it is obvious that you should have served chicken as you originally planned.

These absurd twists in reasoning are generally offered as ways of avoiding banality and snap judgments. They are pseudo-thoughtful, as in *The Fallacy of the Fallacy of First Impressions*, which holds that, despite popular belief, first impressions are often erroneous and misleading. By deft logic, one logical stereotype is replaced by another. In *The Fallacy of the Larger Significance*, whatever explanations and theories are presented are automatically discounted, because they miss out on the larger context. This fallacy, and most of the others, are reversible, since they play on meaningless logical categories. Thus, if you do finally insist on the *Larger Significance*, you may be committing the *Fallacy of the Insignificant Detail*, in which, blinded by the larger meanings, you completely overlook the most obvious fact (for example, that the woman you are courting is married or only pregnant).

Finally, there is the supreme *Fallacy That All Noncomprehension Is Basically Auricular*. In other words, anyone who doesn't understand what you are saying doesn't actually hear what you are saying or is feigning deafness, on the principle that to hear is to understand. We have all had the experience of shouting at foreigners in an attempt to force comprehension. This may be part of the low cunning generally attributed to non-English-speaking peoples, but failure to understand is almost always taken as a form of personal insult, so that the postulation of a hearing problem helps to relieve the anxieties of the speaker.

One much-exploited device of artful nonsense is to attribute banalities to famous persons. In this way, Shakespeare figures importantly in the jestbooks of his time. Most of our presidents either uttered, or are supposed to have uttered, some unforgettable platitude. President Harding is reputed to have cut through the complications of economic theory with this insight: "When there are no jobs, unemployment results." Gerald Ford when Vice-President actually did say: "Whenever a person is called upon to make a speech, the first question that enters his mind is 'What shall I talk about?'" And President Nixon is remembered for having formulated a prophetically sinister analysis of honesty in public life: "Sure there are dishonest men in local government. But there are dishonest men in national government too." Old jokes can be reformulated with a new cast of literary celebrities. Thus, John Keats is sitting at a bar quietly sipping a Pernod when Oscar Wilde enters in a purple suit and asks: "What is all you know or need to know?"

Academic nonsense is in high repute as a way of deflating pretensions. Solemnly stated platitudes are the great specialty of professors, banalities so crushing that it is impossible to greet them with a willing suspension of disbelief. For example, a professor of French literature used to exclaim at the beginning of his course: "The eighteenth century grows out of the seventeenth century and completes it." This solemn pronouncement was made with smugness and finality in French, it was then written on the blackboard, and then spoken again in English, while the professor's ill-fitting dentures clicked off each syllable like the amplified clock of a quiz show. The statement was repeated two or three times a week with an air of mounting frenzy, as if there were just a few moments left to make this one essential point before the world would be destroyed by atomic attack. Students sat in anticipatory terror as the Senior Preceptor—that was his title, unlike any other in the academic establishment—prepared to strike again with his death-dealing platitude.

With malicious parody, Terry Southern and Mason Hoffenberg begin *Candy* (1964) in an academic context, with Professor Mephesto lecturing to his college class:

> "I've read *many* books," said Professor Mephesto, with an odd finality, wearily flattening his hands on the podium, addressing the seventy-six sophomores who sat in easy reverence, immortalizing his every phrase with their pads and pens, and now, as always, giving him the confidence to slowly, artfully dramatize his words, to pause, shrug, frown, gaze abstractly at the ceiling, allow a wan wistful smile to play at his lips, and repeat quietly, "*many* books. . . ." A grave nod of his magnificent head, and he continued: "Yes, and in my time I've traveled widely. They say travel broadens one—and I've . . . no doubt that it does."

The pauses are theatrically rendered, almost like a burlesque of

Pinter, and Professor Mephesto's grand, rhetorical period ends
with a crashing platitude, expressed with all the unctuous overemphasis of *Special Significance:*

> his lip curled in a strange, almost angry way, and a tremor
> came into his voice, while in the lecture hall, not even a
> breath was heard, "I have never seen *anything* . . . to
> *compare* . . . with the *beauty* . . . of the . . . *human face!*"

Professor Mephesto is a philosopher of the *Ladies' Home Journal* and
Cosmopolitan school, and *Candy* merrily explodes the romantic and
pornographic clichés of middlebrow culture.

Banality can have an extraordinary effect, especially if accom-
panied by some physical impediment (real or feigned), like stutter-
ing or a harelip, to give it an entirely gratuitous emphasis. Samuel
Johnson's parody of Bishop Percy's ballad, "The Hermit of Wark-
worth," is a superb example of its kind, and it shows Dr. Johnson's
withering contempt for false simplicity:

> *I put my hat upon my head*
>   *And walked into the Strand,*
> *And there I met another man*
>   *With his hat in his hand.*

Wordsworth misquotes (and somewhat spoils) this stanza in his
Preface to *Lyrical Ballads* (1800), all the while mistakenly insisting
that not the style, but only "the *matter*" is "contemptible." How
perfectly uneventful this little poem is, what mastery it demonstrates of the low mimetic mode! *Multum in parvo*, much in little,
and *via trita, via tuta*, the beaten path is the safe one. No false emphasis there, no spurious attempt to achieve climax, but everywhere a harmonious relation of ends and means in a faultless urban
pastoral.

In an essay on the Rumanian writer I. L. Caragiale, "probably
the greatest of the unknown dramatists," Ionesco calls attention to
his absolute mastery of the banal: "Caragiale's chief originality is
that all his characters are imbeciles . . . sinking completely into

the irrationality of cretinism." This is revealing, since Ionesco himself tried to use cretinism in his early plays to convey the fascinating
stultification of social life. In *The Bald Soprano,* an English couple,
the Martins, while sitting together in the Smiths' living room, ear-
nestly question one another about the details of their personal
life. After each new revelation of all the things they have in common, Mr. Martin exclaims: "How curious it is, good Lord, how
bizarre! And what a coincidence!" Slowly, piece by piece, it is
revealed that they live in the same house, have identical children,
sleep in the same bed, and are actually man and wife. Ionesco carries off this conversation with wonderful high spirits, and the startling conclusion is not more nor less startling than anything else in
the dialogue. Since the couple are, after all, man and wife, why
should it surprise them that they live in the same house, have identical children, and sleep in the same bed? Ionesco's genius for banality is matched by Jonathan Swift's brilliant travesty, *A Compleat
Collection of Genteel and Ingenious Conversation* (1738), where the trite,
proverbial sayings fly thick and fast in the sample dialogues, as in
the following:

> LORD SPARKISH. Pray, my lady Smart, what kin are you to
> lord Pozz?
> LADY SMART. Why, his grandmother and mine had
> four elbows.

Tag lines, or hackneyed, proverbial formulas and catch-
phrases—nuggets of folk wisdom or faded epigrammatic wit—are
becoming rare in American speech, as we strive for a more authentic and personal utterance. In parting from their nephews, uncles
are no longer inclined to say: "Don't take any wooden nickels."
This may be almost as uncommon as the exclamation "Pshaw,"
which is rarely heard in an authentic setting, and certainly seldom
pronounced on all the consonants, as it would be by a real
pshawist. Military speech, on the level of orderly-room colloquial,
uses a certain sprinkling of verbal formulas, some unprintable (like
"How're they hanging?") but all with the logical complexity of "six
of one, half dozen of the other." Most of our current tag lines are

histrionic and jokey, without the innocent, country amusement of "Think it'll get dark tonight?" The melodramatic phrase "We can't go on meeting like this" comes to mind out of the half-world of daytime serials. "Anyone for tennis?" may be more colloquial, but almost any tag line is now associated with commercials, even the seemingly innocuous "I see you're admiring my shoes" (or tie, hat, watch-fob, etc.).

Some tag lines clearly originate with stand-up comics, especially "How'm I doing so far?" and "Is there a doctor in the house?" or even "Hi, Mom" (which was the title of a hilarious Brian de Palma movie). British tag lines are closely connected with music hall, and some, such as "How's your mother fixed for drippings?" are mystifying to an American. Traditionally, tag lines have built-in sexual innuendos regardless of the literal meanings of the words, since they are uttered during embarrassing pauses in the conversation to fill, as it were, gaps in the dialogue. "Does your mother know you're out?" sparks off a whole series of questions for which any member of the family may be substituted. For example, "Does your stepfather know you're out?" or "Does your cousin know you're out?" The humor, if there is any, is subtle and impenetrable.

Tag lines can be strung together with various filler words and phrases to imply a spurious sense of continuity. "*And* how's your uncle?" Or, "And, by the way, how's your aunt?" These questions, unrelated to anything that precedes or follows, are supposed to make listeners vaguely uneasy, like double-talk. Something is going on outside their dim comprehension, "and Bob's your uncle," "*paucas palabras,*" "let the world slip," "we are young only once," and "a word to the wise is sufficient." Hamlet's advice to the Clown (as recorded only in the First—and Bad—Quarto of 1603) has some enigmatic tag lines that he warns the Clown against repeating. "Cannot you stay till I eat my porridge?" "you owe me / A quarter's wages," and "your beer is sour." It's a great puzzle to know either why these lines were once funny or why it is so important for Hamlet to prevent the Clown from speaking them. They may not be tag lines at all, but some variety of fossilized punch lines from gags that were making the rounds in the year 1603.

Comic aimlessness and stupidity create the illusion of naive, unconscious humor.

The logic of non sequiturs lends itself to larger units of nonsense, especially aimless discourse, meandering and pointless, full of elaborate (but irrelevant) specifications and qualifications that are endlessly proliferated without advancing—or in any way touching upon—any real or imagined subject. Perhaps this is in the tradition of the tall—or at least elongated—tale, or a form of the shaggy-dog story, but even a shaggy-dog story moves inexorably toward its shattering anticlimax, while the infinitely winding talk I have in mind never reaches any conclusion at all.

Dame Quickly's interrogation of Falstaff in the presence of the Lord Chief Justice offers a good example of the vivid distractibility of the human reason:

> Thou didst swear to me upon a parcel-gilt [partly gilded] goblet, sitting in my Dolphin chamber, at the round table, by a sea-coal fire, upon Wednesday in Wheeson [Whitsun] week, when the Prince broke thy head for liking [likening] his father to a singing-man of Windsor, thou didst swear to me then, as I was washing thy wound, to marry me and make me my lady thy wife. Canst thou deny it? Did not goodwife Keech, the butcher's wife, come in then and call me gossip Quickly? Coming in to borrow a mess of vinegar, telling us she had a good dish of prawns, whereby thou didst desire to eat some, whereby I told thee they were ill for a green [fresh] wound? (*Henry IV, Part 2* 2.1.87–100)

The truth is hopelessly muddled and compromised by Dame Quickly's total recall of the occasion, and at the end of her discourse we are still not properly at the beginning of an answer to Falstaff's question: "What is the gross sum that I owe thee?" (2.1.85).

There is a more grandiose example in Ionesco's *The Bald Soprano*, which is more properly nonsensical and frenetic in the best traditions of surrealism. It is the Fire Chief's story called "The Head-cold," which I will quote in its entirety so as not to lose any of the excruciating details:

> My brother-in-law had, on the paternal side, a first cousin whose maternal uncle had a father-in-law whose paternal grandfather had married as his second wife a young native whose brother he had met on one of his travels, a girl of whom he was enamored and by whom he had a son who married an intrepid lady pharmacist who was none other than the niece of an unknown fourth-class petty officer of the Royal Navy and whose adopted father had an aunt who spoke Spanish fluently and who was, perhaps, one of the granddaughters of an engineer who died young, himself the grandson of the owner of a vineyard which produced mediocre wine, but who had a second cousin, a stay-at-home, a sergeant-major, whose son had married a very pretty young woman, a divorcée, whose first husband was the son of a loyal patriot who, in the hope of making his fortune, had managed to bring up one of his daughters so that she could marry a footman who had known Rothschild, and whose brother, after having changed his trade several times, married and had a daughter whose stunted great-grandfather wore spectacles which had been given him by a cousin of his, the brother-in-law of a man from Portugal, natural son of a miller, not too badly off, whose foster-brother had married the daughter of a former country doctor, who was himself a foster-brother of the son of a forester, himself the natural son of another country doctor, married three times in a row, whose third wife . . . was the daughter of the best midwife in the region and who, early left a widow, . . . had married a glazier who was full of life and who had had, by the daughter of a station master, a child who had burned his bridges . . . and had married an oyster woman, whose father had a brother, mayor of a small town, who had taken as his wife a blonde schoolteacher, whose cousin, a fly fisherman . . . had married another blonde schoolteacher,

named Marie, too, whose brother was married to another
Marie, also a blonde schoolteacher . . . and whose father
had been reared in Canada by an old woman who was the
niece of a priest whose grandmother, occasionally in the
winter, like everyone else, caught a cold.

As Mrs. Smith comments, "A curious story. Almost unbelievable,"
and completely in the spirit of the celebrated final sentence of the
psychiatrist in Philip Roth's priapic novel, *Portnoy's Complaint:* "So
[*said the doctor*]. Now vee may perhaps to begin. Yes?"

In Shakespeare's *Much Ado About Nothing*, Dogberry and Verges,
the Keystone Cops of their generation, hack their way through the
thick undergrowth of language to make a difficult, if not impossible, exposition, as in Dogberry's fearless answer to the villainous
prisoner Conrade:

Dost thou not suspect my place? Dost thou not suspect my
years? O that he were here to write me down an ass! But,
master, remember that I am an ass. Though it be not
written down, yet forget not that I am an ass. No, thou
villain, thou art full of piety, as shall be proved upon thee
by good witness. (4.2.75–80)

Dogberry and Verges sprinkle malapropisms thickly about them—
especially Dogberry's inimitable "Comparisons are odorous"
(3.5.16)—although the rhetorical device is properly named for
Sheridan's Mrs. Malaprop in *The Rivals* (1775), whose "progeny of
learning," "very pineapple of politeness," and "as headstrong as an
allegory on the banks of the Nile" are vivaciously metaphorical.

Malapropisms require a certain genius, and, like the aimless discourse noticed above, they are always the ironic formations of a
sophisticated author for his "low" characters. There may be natural, spontaneous, even accidental malapropisms, but they are relatively few compared to the weight of literary malapropism. The
humorous errors attributed to peasants and rustics sound more like
sly put-ons than innocent and spontaneous utterances. Thus, Cor-
sican peasants are not supposed to understand the highfalutin word
"banale" (banal), which they regularly render as "banane" (banana).

But "c'est banane," or "it's bananas," as we might say, sounds suspiciously familiar. "Bananas" is a slang word for crazy, as in Woody Allen's movie of that name, and "to go bananas" is the equivalent of the Army phrase, "to go ape." Apes, of course, particularly like bananas, so there's the missing link to connect the two expressions. The old songs, "Yes, We Have No Bananas" and "I Like Bananas Because They Have No Bones," are also part of the same connotational system.

Even the related device of spoonerism, which Wyld, in his *Universal Dictionary*, defines as "involuntary transposition of sounds in successive words" (for example, *"queer dean"* for *dear queen"*), seems suspicious and not so involuntary as Wyld suggests, nor is his example without suspiciously fortuitous overtones. Comic metathesis, no matter how well intended, comes under the general rules for slips of the tongue that Freud laid down in his *Psychopathology of Everyday Life* (1904). Our slips are always revealing, and there is no such thing as a completely involuntary slip—just various degrees of conscious awareness of what we really wanted to say.

Many boners are not so innocent as they seem, but are rather the crafty creations of cunning schoolboys trying to put their teachers on—or maybe of the teachers themselves, who are, after all, our chief source of documentation. *The Pocket Book of Boners*, culled from various Viking Press collections (1931–32), has the subtitle: *An Omnibus of Schoolboy Howlers and Unconscious Humor*, in which "unconscious" is undoubtedly a better word than Wyld's "involuntary." Some of these boners echo standard jokes or conundrums, such as: "Who have more fun than infants in infancy? Adults in adultery." All the best ones have an air of sophisticated nonsense about them that is a tribute to the ingenuity of wit rather than the hilarious blundering of naivety. A favorite is: "A virgin forest is a forest in which the hand of man has never set foot." The wildly mixed metaphors have an energy all their own, and they plumb the heights of the depths.

To the purist, popular violations of Latin usage like "rather unique" and "four or five alternatives" are equally ridiculous. Or what are we to make of the phrase "a bit pregnant"? "Pregnant" is clearly a predicate that cannot take the partitive but welcomes parturition. The section on definitions in *The Pocket Book of Boners* is the most successful part of the book, since definitions demand a certain comprehensiveness as well as lucidity: "Aesophagus was the author of Aesop's Fables." "The artichoke was an ancient instrument of torture." "A sirloin is the only article of clothing worn by Gandhi, the leader of India." These examples have a feeling for metaphor, and the dead metaphors concealed in literal language spring to life again.

The following examples sound like the standard gags one hears on television, especially on shows like the now defunct *Laugh-In*, where the speed of delivery tended to mask the extreme artfulness of the stupidity. "A millenium is something like a centennial, only it has more legs." "Mastication is what the Italians do with their hands when they talk English"—that's definitely off-color. "Strategy is when you don't let the enemy know you are out of ammunition, but keep on firing." Or, for a pungent example not in the *Pocket Book* collection: "McCormick invented the automatic raper, which could do the work of a thousand men in one day." The use of the word "work" suggests the sophistication of the gag writer; this cannot be a genuine folk example. To do boners well demands Socratic irony so that you can convince your audience that you are fighting your way to the dim light of comprehension. Needless to say, ingenuousness is a difficult role to sustain, and unintended foolishness always seems less funny than unintended seriousness.

Out of the mouths of babes shall come wisdom, not jokes, and we lack well authenticated sources of naive humor. We are coming to the sad realization that, despite Freud's theories to the contrary, children, peasants, and even schoolboys may be much wittier and more artful than we give them credit for. How are we, for example, to understand the following "true" story about a college student's error on a Shakespeare examination? When asked to identify Mercutio's comment on his death-wound: "No, 'tis not so deep as a well, nor so wide as a church door; but 'tis enough, 'twill serve" (*Romeo and Juliet* 3.1.97–98), the student replied: "This is Romeo speaking about Juliet on their wedding night." The story would sound more genuine if its origin were not attributed to different places of learning throughout our fair land, depending on the teller's own malicious inclinations.

Popular humor is topical and satirical.

The chief source book for the gag writer or stand-up comedian has
always been the newspaper, or, in the days before newspapers and
up-to-the-minute television reports, the gossip that was heard in
the market place, at the baths, in popular drinking places, and in the
public rooms of brothels. Old jokes and bons mots are constantly
being adapted to new situations. Almost as soon as President Ford
had been named to replace Nixon, commentators were quoting
Lyndon Johnson's observation that Gerald Ford was the only man
he knew who couldn't chew gum and walk at the same time, or
that Ford had played football too long without a helmet. During
the postal campaign to stamp out obscene mail, there was a popular
cancellation that said: "Report Obscene Mail to Your Postmaster,"
and vulnerable persons could put their names on an official list of
those who, although over twenty-one, did not wish to receive any
adult-type mail. It was during this difficult period that a button
mysteriously appeared with a piece of practical advice: "Use
Erogenous Zone Numbers." Another said: "Report Obscene Mail
to Your Postmistress." All these postal slogans may stem from the
erotic associations of "Post Office," an adolescent kissing game like
"Spin the Bottle."

The button craze dredged up all kinds of immediate social com-
mentary and social protest, such as: "Make Love, Not War,"
"Draft Beer, Not Students," "Save Water, Shower with a Friend,"
"When This Button Begins to Melt You Know You Are in the
Midst of an Atomic Attack." Among drug-related slogans were the
following: "Acid Indigestion? Check Your Source" (a parody of the
Jest stomach-tablet commercial), "Peanut Butter Is Better than
Pot," "Mary Poppins Is a Junkie." The wearing of topical buttons
replaced the commonplace book as a source of epigrammatic and
very temporary wit, and many of the buttons gave advice on lifestyle and ultimate values: "Jesus Saves, Moses Invests," "Dress British, Think Yiddish," "One Man's Oud Is Another Man's Mandolin," "Just Because You're Paranoid Doesn't Mean that They're
Not Out to Get You," and the enigmatic "Thimk." One of the
most metaphysical was a declaration from the student movement:

"Notice: Tomorrow Has Been Cancelled Due to Lack of Interest."

The graffiti in toilets, especially men's rooms (although this may be an ignorant male chauvinist's attitude on the matter), have always been considered the best source for topical humor, since they are periodically scrubbed, repainted, or just simply crossed out by persons with more urgent messages. There is an excellent collection of these graffiti by the philologist Allen Walker Read, culled from men's rooms in the western National Parks, under the disarming title: *Lexical Evidence from Folk Epigraphy in Western North America: A Glossorial Study of the Low Element in the English Vocabulary* (Paris, privately printed, 1935). Beneath the Ionesco facade of phonology lurks a little classic of pornography, and Read's examples are highly traditional, some even echoing graffiti found in the ruins of Pompeii.

One of the most insistent personae of graffiti is the scoffer at all inscriptions, as in the familiar couplet: "A man's ambition must be pretty small, / To write his name [or his thoughts, or his poetry] on a toilet wall." Or the obscure, esoteric, ultimately unanswerable question: "Why are you looking up here?" Army inscriptions are often answers to endless, stenciled directives; for example, "Do Not Throw Butts in the Urinals" continues: "Because It Makes Them Wet and Soggy and Hard to Smoke." Or "We Aim To Keep This Place Clean" leads to the inevitable "Your Aim Will Help," which is sometimes crowned with an additional comment: "The Next Guy Who Comes in Here May Have Holes in His Shoes," followed by an indignant exclamation: "I Was That Guy, You Bastard!"

When a hot-air hand dryer was installed in the student men's room in Scott Hall at Rutgers University (which still maintains a separate but equal faculty men's room, much less rich in scholia), a penciled direction appeared: "Press This Button and Hear a Speech by Richard Nixon." An elaborate system of arrows soon rerouted this direction to the handle of the flushometer, with its anticipated, vacuum-breaking gurgles. Among various other moral and immoral comments is the stoic injunction: "Your Fate Is in Your Hands," with the *e* of "fate" sometimes scratched out. Hopeless warnings fill the walls and partitions (in the genre of confessional literature): "No Use in Standing Up; The Crabs in This Toilet Can Jump Ten

Feet," or the touching revelation: "It Was Only Too Late That I Discovered the TRUTH: Self-Abuse Leads to Madness."

Is this naive, spontaneous humor, or do the anonymous authors remember clever, epigrammatic sayings they have seen elsewhere? Statistics tend to support the latter notion, since graffiti, like jokes, are a folk product that no known individual ever consciously composes, although they may be falsely attributed to famous persons. The rash of Confucius jokes some years ago had nothing whatsoever to do with oriental wisdom; for example, "Confucius say: Piano player who play downbeat wrong get beat up." These derive from and progress into "knock-knock, who's there" jokes, moron jokes, and the jests of well known, historical comedians or comic personalities, such as Tarlton, Armin, Joe Miller, Graf Bubi, etc. It is as if a single, immutable body of material is infinitely edited, reworked, varied, and brought up-to-date, and that the process will continue for ever.

The basic premise is that everything connected with respectable, decent, orderly, middle-class society is subject to ridicule, the more outrageous the better. Satire of accepted norms and standards is an almost automatic impulse, but one may well question the old assumption that the satirist really calls us to our senses, rather than merely poking fun at our collective foibles. Did the "hang-out route" or the "semi-hang-out route" (otherwise called truth and public exposure) really do in Richard Nixon and his associates and laugh them out of office? We should question the practical efficacy of satire and the reformist motives of the satirist, who usually wants to take credit for results achieved by righteous indignation and public zeal.

During the dirty words phase of the student movement at Berkeley, the mere utterance of dirty words was supposed to be the height of satirical wit and to bring down the Establishment. There is nothing more pitiful than to see someone who pretends to wit wearing a button that says only "cunnilingus" (and not its academic equivalent, "cunning linguist"). More topically, during the infamously swift events of the "Saturday Night Massacre," Nixon's dismissal of Archibald Cox earned him the title of "Nixon the Cox Sacker." Full frontal assault is not the same thing as political satire. A determined practitioner can make his point by wearing a button with Chester Alan Arthur's picture (distributed gratis by the Federated Chester Alan Arthur Clubs of North America), who was, after all, our most beautiful president, or by playing poker with a deck of Ulysses S. Grant cards. Satirical understatement is still statement, and he who laughs loudest is not necessarily the one who is heard (as Confucius say).

Condensation and an epigrammatic style are essential aspects of comic creativity.

Many of the qualities that Freud attributes to jokes and dreams are those of creativity in general, and especially creativity in words. Freud's theories of displacement and condensation concern the workings of the imaginative process and should not be limited either to jokes or dreams. The dreamer and the teller of jokes work on the raw materials of daily life, and certain preoccupying images are displaced, refashioned, and given a new sequence and emphasis in the dream or joke, which is in itself a condensed and highly wrought work of art. The fact that much of this process takes place with remarkable speed and without conscious volition should not affect our judgment of the results, which may be good or bad according to aesthetic criteria.

The most fascinating witticism in Freud's book on jokes also happens to be the one that is most condensed: "A wife is like an umbrella—sooner or later one takes a cab." The form of the joke is epigrammatic. It seems to be making an essential definition in a witty, polished, and paradoxical style, and the definition form allies it with the tradition of bons mots and/or boners (depending upon whether the humor is intended or unintended, if one could ever precisely determine that distinction). But what does it mean, and is the proposition stated in such a reduced form that its meaning is unintelligible?

Freud's explanation is unforgettable: "One marries in order to protect oneself against the temptations of sensuality, but it turns out nevertheless that marriage does not allow of the satisfaction of needs that are somewhat stronger than usual. In just the same way, one takes an umbrella with one to protect oneself from the rain and nevertheless gets wet in the rain. In both cases one must look around for a stronger protection: in the latter case one must take a public vehicle, and in the former a woman who is accessible in return for money." An umbrella is, of course, a powerful phallic symbol, especially in its capacity to open (either manually or automatically), and we know from Ernest Jones's biography that Freud loathed umbrellas. This colors the sexuality of the joke, which needs all the covert support it can get to enunciate a point Freud considered very delicate: "One does not venture to declare aloud and openly that marriage is not an arrangement calculated to satisfy a man's sexuality." The joke is becoming progressively more personal, barbed, and defensive, and it echoes the folk wisdom attributed to Kipling: "A woman is only a woman, but a good cigar is a smoke."

The epigrammatic style permeates jokes and joke-telling. The condensed, polished, and perfected form of the epigram is an expression of classic wit. One internal and historical irony is that epigrams have usually been extremely scurrilous: directed specifically and maliciously against persons and their failings, especially physical ones, such as impotence, ugliness, deformity, bodily odors, and personal uncleanness. The brief stanza (usually no more than two lines, but sometimes four or more) tempts the writer to a single, stunning blow, generally aimed at the subject's moral character and pretensions to respectability.

The Roman poet Martial (of the first century A.D.) wrote about 1500 epigrams, ranging from gentle fun to stinging insult. The following, in Rolfe Humphries' colloquial translation, is fairly mild:

> *Paula, it comes to me as no surprise*
> *You want to marry Priscus; you are wise.*
> *But Priscus doesn't want to marry you,*
> *Which goes to prove, I'd say, that he's wise, too.*

But the next is more characteristically barbed:

> *Lesbia swears she never was laid for free.*
> *Correct—she always had to pay the fee.*

The point of the epigram as a poetic vehicle is to demonstrate the fine control you can exercise over your energetic malice. Strong feeling is mastered by wit and a vigorously concise style.

The best English epigrams are by Robert Herrick, a lyric poet of the seventeenth century, who imitates the sensuous grace and barbed wit of classical poets such as Catullus and Horace. Herrick can be playful and coy, as in this couplet:

> *Maids' nays are nothing; they are shy*
> *But to desire what they deny.*

The antithetic twist takes the reader by surprise, and that is the purpose of its sudden wit, as in the sly quatrain on Slouch:

> *Slouch he packs up and goes to several fairs*
> *And weekly markets for to sell his wares.*
> *Meantime that he from place to place does roam,*
> *His wife her own ware sells as fast at home.*

Herrick's scurrilous epigrams are much more frank and energetic:

> *Scobble for whoredom whips his wife, and cries*
> *He'll slit her nose. But blubbering she replies,*
> *"Good sir, make no more cuts i' th' outward skin;*
> *One slit's enough to let adultery in."*

The scornful couplet on Suds, a laundress, is engagingly nasty and tawdry:

> *Suds launders bands [a kind of collar] in piss, and starches them*
> *Both with her husband's and her own tough phlegm.*

Many epigrams are not, of course, comic, but the shortness and pithiness of the form and its balanced structure lend themselves to a sudden, strong climax. We are meant to admire the verve and the brilliance of the poet's vituperation.

The epigrammatic style extends far beyond the writing of verse epigrams, and it is probably the chief characteristic of what we now call wit. We may define the epigrammatic style fully and formally as: A cool, calculated, detached attitude, combined with mastery of the ironic, malicious, cutting retort, which is composed with full command of paradox, metaphoric condensation, and polished antitheses and is spoken with exquisite politeness and sympathetic charm. Oscar Wilde is the great artist of this style, and *The Importance of Being Earnest* is perhaps the most consistently epigrammatic work in the English language. Comedy of manners lends itself to the vilification (or mock-vilification, since there are no serious attitudes at all—that would be out of keeping with the tone) of middle-class values and comfortable, Victorian mores. The very title plays on the name Ernest and all the rebarbative bourgeois attitudes implied in "being earnest."

When Lady Bracknell questions Jack on his qualifications as a prospective husband, she is delighted to learn that Jack smokes: "I am glad to hear it. A man should always have an occupation of some kind. There are far too many idle men in London as it is." She also admires the fact that he claims to "know nothing": "I am pleased to hear it. I do not approve of anything that tampers with natural ignorance. Ignorance is like a delicate exotic fruit; touch it and the bloom is gone." It is all beautifully paradoxical, and Wilde's idle, useless, insouciant, upper-class speakers mock their own attitudinizing as vigorously as the official objects of their epigrammatic disdain. Despite his reformist emphasis, Shaw seems to have learned a good deal from Wilde, especially about language as the primary instrument in the social struggle. The Socialist program becomes a battle of wits, and Shaw's spokesmen are always masters of the intellectual epigram. Tom Stoppard is in the same tradition, with a wilder, more uninhibited, and more specifically parodistic style.

In the popular, democratic tradition, the limerick replaces the epigram as a witty, topical/satirical verse form, with a special penchant for pornographic anapests, dactyls, and feminine rhymes. Everyone almost without exception knows some dirty limericks (or at least some nonsensical ones), which can be made to appear, like invisible writing, by soaking in alcohol. The wit of the limerick softens the barbs, and we admire the brilliance while we chuckle at the malicious point. The multiple rhymes of a successful limerick tame (or at least tease) its unpleasant subject, and there is an ironic contrast between the grossness of the subject and the surprising skill and lightness of the poetic style, as in the following:

> *There once was a whore [pronounced "who-a" in lower-class New*
>   *York speech] from Rockaway,*
> *Who you could smell from a block away,*
>   *I took one whiff,*
>   *And I got the syph,*
> *And now it's eating my cock away.*

There are many variations, some more or less authentic, but it is important to get the mingled effect of a disgusting theme handled with poetic charm.

Many limericks, especially those of Edward Lear and Carolyn Wells, are actually nonsense verses that turn on linguistic and orthographic puzzles. We are meant to admire the ingenuity of the writer and his admirable cleverness, as in the following from Untermeyer's *Lots of Limericks*:

> *She frowned and called him Mr.*
> *Because in sport he kr.*
>   *And so in spite*
>   *That very nite*
> *This Mr. kr. sr.*

Once we have worked out the phonetic equivalents of the abbreviations, we realize that, in full spelling, this is an unremarkable poem that depends entirely on tricks. The following ethnic limerick has teasing feminine rhymes:

> *A pious old Jew from Salonika,*
> *Said "For Christmas I'd like a harmonica."*
>   *His wife, to annoy him,*
>   *Said, "Feh! That's for goyim!"*
> *And gave him a jews-harp for Chanukah.*

The rhymes are outrageous, even macaronic ("annoy him/*goyim*"), and we are delighted to be entertained with such panache.

Perfect timing is the ideal all actors and joke-tellers are striving to achieve.

Rhetoric ultimately depends on the ability to produce effects, and comic rhetoric needs to move its auditors to laughter, or at least to a feeling of amusement and mirth. I am not convinced that comedy may be only a state of mind separate and abstracted from its psychological and physiological symptoms. Since comedy is such an intrinsically oral art, it is dependent on the time element for its effects. Comedians tend to be masters of delay, of deliberately slowing down the movement of a joke or a narrative—virtually losing themselves in perverse irrelevancies—until they suddenly, and at exactly the right moment, press in with the climax or punch line. Timing in comedy achieves remarkable effects of surprise and wonder that have nothing to do with the subject matter but are essentially aesthetic. It is not so much the joke that is funny, but the whole experience of listening to the joke, and, therefore, what we read on paper is only an echo of the joke. There is, after all, a sharp distinction between comedian and gag writer, between actor and dramatist. Properly speaking, the joke can only be a temporal experience created by a narrator and the audience. Everything else is an imitation, and, despite the authority of Plato and the Platonic doctrine of mimesis, we are not inclined to accept imitations.

Comedy works in time (or duration), and timing is the high art of controlling the passage of time, either speeding it up or slowing it down for some calculated purpose. Actors think of timing as the most profound mystery of all. It is not enough just to speak lines; pace, tempo, emphasis, and an intuitive grasp of movement are needed to make the lines come alive. For the joke-teller, it is essential to master the audience. Once that occurs, anything told will be funny. With a perfect sense of timing, the joke-teller can instinctively feel the right rhythm for the delivery, and whether to give more or less at any particular moment. The joke is not a fixed form, and that is why purposive and subject-matter theories of comedy are almost by their very nature defective. Nothing is intrinsically comic; to make others laugh is a triumph of the will.

A typical Shakespearean technique is to have his comic heroes emerge from their context, to step out boldly from their back-

ground and assume an autonomous identity. In *Love's Labor's Lost*,
for example, Costard the clown suddenly steals the show during
the play of the Nine Worthies. As the other amateur actors falter in
their parts, Costard intervenes to apologize for them. Of Nathaniel
the curate, stagestruck as Alexander the Great, Costard explains:
"a foolish mild man; an honest man, look you, and soon dashed.
He is a marvelous good neighbor, faith, and a very good bowler;
but for Alisander—alas! you see how 'tis—a little o'erparted"
(5.2.579–83). Costard is completely at his ease, without any irritating, ironic sense of distinction between being an actor and being a
commentator on the play. His timing is perfect and he can do no
wrong; he is a natural actor.

Shakespeare knew that his clown-comedians might take over the
play if given the opportunity. That is why, in Hamlet's advice to
the players, Hamlet is so anxious to prevent the clowns from ad-
libbing:

> "And let those that play your clowns speak no more than
> is set down for them, for there be of them that will
> themselves laugh, to set on some quantity of barren
> spectators to laugh too, though in the meantime some
> necessary question of the play be then to be considered."
> (3.2.40–45)

Hamlet is very serious about plays (and the capacity of a play to
catch the conscience of a king), so that we shouldn't automatically
equate his special views about clowns with those of Shakespeare.

The autonomous clown, speaking directly to the audience, is
fairly common in Shakespeare, especially in the earlier plays.
Launce in *The Two Gentlemen of Verona* has an elaborate soliloquy in
which he describes his maudlin parting from his family, and he ac-
cuses his dog Crab, who is on stage with him, of not shedding a
single tear. With perfect ease and composure, Launce lays out the
scene for the audience:

> "This shoe is my father; no, this left shoe is my father.
> No, no, this left shoe is my mother; nay, that cannot be so
> neither. Yes, it is so, it is so, it hath the worser sole. This

shoe, with the hole in it, is my mother, and this my
father; a vengeance on't! There 'tis." (2.3.15–20)

This quote is the beginning of a very typical clown's routine, with
its bad pun ("sole/soul") and off-color joke (mother's hole), but it is
almost unintelligible without the mugging and broad gestures that
accompany the identification of shoes.

There is nothing in any way droll in the mere words of the
monologue: "This shoe is my father; no, this left shoe is my father
. . . ," and we are at a terrible disadvantage to have to read it
barely on the printed page. The following bit with the dog seems
just as blank when we try to interpret it cold, without its nonverbal
context: "I am the dog. No, the dog is himself, and I am the dog.
Oh! The dog is me, and I am myself; ay, so, so" (2.3.22–24). As a
piece of acting, however, it is a beautiful study in comic stupidity,
and it offers the clown a marvelous opportunity to give the audience a "taste of his quality."

Comic art is aesthetic, and it works within its own characteristic
idiom of dramatic time. A studied ease and composure are essential
for the comic performer, who is always conscious of being an actor
playing a role. That is the secret of Falstaff's great success: he is
never sincere or personal, but always performing for the world at
large. The revelation of his cowardice in the robbery at Gadshill,
engineered by Prince Hal and Poins, means nothing at all to Falstaff, who, caught in the act of lying, answers with perfect aplomb:

> "By the Lord, I knew ye as well as he that made ye. Why,
> hear you, my masters. Was it for me to kill the heir
> apparent? Should I turn upon the true prince? Why, thou
> knowest I am as valiant as Hercules, but beware instinct.
> The lion will not touch the true prince. Instinct is a great
> matter. I was now a coward on instinct." (*Henry IV, Part 1*
> 2.4.268–74)

Falstaff is not so easily discombobulated as other men, because he
is not touched by truth or falsehood. In his world, only wit has validity.

When, in the same scene, he plays King Henry to Hal's Falstaff, he does it with perfect mastery of tone and style:

> "Harry, I do not only marvel where thou spendest thy
> time, but also how thou art accompanied. For though the
> camomile, the more it is trodden on, the faster it grows, so
> youth, the more it is wasted, the sooner it wears. That
> thou art my son I have partly thy mother's word, partly
> my own opinion, but chiefly a villainous trick of thine eye
> and a foolish hanging of thy nether lip that doth warrant
> me." (2.4.398–405)

How gracefully Falstaff dabbles in the courtly, euphuistic style, so foreign to his ordinary speech, and decorates his discourse with unnatural natural history, polished antitheses, and suspended syntax. He does it all with true aristocratic negligence, and neither the King, nor his sons, nor his courtiers ever match Falstaff's regal style. Henry IV is king by divine right; Falstaff by temporal and histrionic assertion. Falstaff plays the king in time and for a limited time only, but in the world of comedy to play the king is a more notable accomplishment than to be the king.

II

Comic
Characters:
Conventions
and
Types

By natural impulse, comedy is conventional, firmly anchored in type characters and stock situations. This is not to say that comedy doesn't seek out originality and even wildness, but only that originality and wildness are produced by the handling of the comic materials rather than by the materials themselves. This may be a quibble, since ends and means, form and content tend to merge and become indistinguishable, but comedy retains its traditional character even when it seems most novel and eccentric. There is an underlying set of assumptions that is readily understood by both audience and playwright.

Comedy prefers a simplified and schematized psychology, derived from received ideas about comic characterization rather than from the rough and tumble of daily life. Comedy has a full set of potential characters, who exist outside any particular time and place, although they may be influenced by the writer's own society. The so-called "realism" of comedy needs to be strongly qualified. To use comic materials for the purpose of social documentation, as some historians and literary critics do, necessarily involves distortion. L. C. Knights's *Drama and Society in the Age of Jonson* (1937) is a rich and subtle book, but the presence of money-grubbing usurers in English plays of the early seventeenth century may just as convincingly be attributed to the influence of Roman comedy as to the economic pressures of a newly turbulent moneyed class in Jacobean England.

Some of the practical implications of comic conventions and the tradition of comic types will be explored in this chapter, especially the comfortable and familiar feeling we receive from comedy: that everything is for the best in this best of all possible worlds. We feel at home in comedy even when the characters seem to be anarchic, destructive, and revolutionary. We are therefore confident that all impulses, no matter how negative, come from characters whose heart is in the right place and whose good will is going to be validated by the happy ending. It is difficult to escape from the prevailingly optimistic tone.

Conventions are a tacit agreement between playwright and audience about social stereotypes and the ways of representing them.

Comedy deals in stereotypes rather than fully rounded, three-dimensional, living characters, just as much of social life is conducted by stereotypes rather than by a fresh, objective appraisal of each situation as it arises. It is possible for those who habitually deal in stereotypes to break loose from their moorings and to engage in fresh appraisals, but the latter is counterpointed against the former. That is, we are conscious of making a special effort for a special case, different from the customary ebb and flow of daily existence. These rules (or rules of thumb) also apply in comedy, where there is continual skirmishing between originality and convention, between the demands of live persons and the easy familiarity of stock types. Great comic characters like Falstaff are both highly original and highly traditional, depending upon what aspect of the character we choose to consider, but the originality is especially striking because of (and not in spite of) the basis in convention.

Comic convention postulates a society that is rigidly hierarchical. By the laws of decorum, carefully formulated by such Roman rhetoricians as Cicero and Quintilian, different social classes have their prescribed styles, both of manners and of speech. The hierarchy is conveniently divided into three major categories: high, middle, and low, although there are also unlimited gradations in between. The high people are lords and ladies, kings and queens, princes, dukes, and other aristocrats, as well as all persons thought vaguely to be "great," either by vast wealth virtuously acquired, or by some other distinction. Thus, if Aristotle or even St. Francis suddenly appeared, we would expect them to speak in the high style appropriate to dignified persons. They might sound a bit bombastic, and certainly very formal, but personal and colloquial touches are excluded from the diction of the high style.

Middle persons are generally people like ourselves, who constitute the vast and almost unbounded middle class in America. They are neither exalted nor base, particularly vicious nor especially virtuous, but only representative types, whose normal reactions may be counted on for comic effect. They define public opinion, what the world thinks, common sense, unexaggerated decency, and unheroic propriety, and they can be relied on to do what is expected of them and not to muck up the works. They speak in the "middle" style of daily discourse, clear and businesslike, but neither personal nor colorful.

Most comic action is generated from low characters, who may

be, most characteristically, servants, but could also be working-men, country rubes, clowns, tramps, unemployables, layabouts, professional beggars, street musicians, jugglers, sellers of patent medicine, or traveling salesmen—the old kind, who traveled about with samples that they sold (which thus allied them with peddlers) and who slept with the farmer's daughter. To this ill-assorted group of misfits and outcasts we may add exiles and escapees from the high and middle classes, who are usually only on detached service with the low people. They are slumming, as it were, temporarily resting from their high responsibilities or postponing the moment when they will be forced to take up their options. Youths on holiday and on the make are evident in this category, pleasantly floating on the island of post-adolescent indulgence. The resolution of the comic action usually brings this idyllic period to an end.

The low characters are generally felt to be classless rather than lower class. Their sociological authenticity might, in fact, get in the way of their comic potential. There is no reason to believe, for example, that migratory agricultural workers are funny; anyone reading the newspaper would tend to think just the reverse. The minstrel-show darkies who sang spirituals on the old plantation after their day's work was done (at least in movies of the 1930s) have no relation whatsoever to real blacks, who are accustomed neither to grin from ear to ear nor to sing in unctuous harmonies—the Inkspots are obviously a parody of what we are talking about. Comedy needs these stereotypes, but we shouldn't blind ourselves to think that they represent some identifiable social reality. The minstrel-show darkie is, by definition, a white man playing a black man and is grotesquely made up to look like one, especially to a white audience. We may also have black men playing black men to white audiences, or to white society in general, but that is a different kind of role-playing from the minstrel-show darkie. We are talking about impersonations and the creation of comic characters, rather than about authentic lower-class life, which might provide a completely untractable basis for comedy. Like real life in general, any subject matter needs to be processed and converted by the comic imagination; as a raw material or natural resource it is not yet usable.

The speech of low characters tends to be unpredictable and outside the expectations of social decorum. It is vivid, colloquial, slangy, pungent, and wild. Talk is an expressive medium rather than one that communicates anything rational. Ideas are more or less banished from this discourse, which moves hyperbolically and by free association. Drink is thought to be helpful in freeing up the association. As the humble Mr. Sousé (vilely mispronounced by his neighbors and townsfolk) in *The Bank Dick*, W. C. Fields talks with a compulsive, but extremely low-keyed and deadpan frenzy, as in his exchange with a gawky, overgrown young man (played by Grady Sutton), who is exceptionally stupid:

> *FIELDS.* My grandfather was a balloon ascensionist, and one day he jumped out of his balloon and took a chance of landing on a load of hay.
> *YOUNG MAN.* But did he make it?
> *FIELDS.* Had he been a younger man, he might have made it. . . .

This is hardly dialogue, in the sense of a mutual exchange of spoken comments. Fields is a talker but not a conversationalist, which is an art that makes social demands beyond the comprehension of a low comic hero, who is a monologuist, a soliloquizer, and a general entertainer of multitudes. The conversationalist listens to what other people are saying because he is polite, is filled with intellectual curiosity, or is merely trying to wear out his opponent. Fields, however, has no concern for what others are saying, even about him. He is grandly egotistical, self-expressive, and flamboyantly personal. He is so admirably suited for comedy because he considers himself a fictional character—which he happens to be. He doesn't have the effrontery to advance any Ibsenish claims for truth and the ideal.

Identity is conventionally defined by external signs, and costume is a significant expression of personality.

In comedy, the question of identity that plays such a large role in tragedy is often reduced to a matter of costume, which defines identity in unambiguous terms. We can have tragedy in street dress or rehearsal dress—perhaps it even helps to get the tragedy out of its historical mold and to universalize its characters and themes—but comedy needs elaborate and fully consistent costumes to make it work. Comedy is so fastidious about costume because, in such a highly conventional form, it is one of the chief means of characterization. The characters are externally defined by occupation, social class, wealth (or absence of it), and even mood and temperament.

A stiff and awkward person will be wearing tight and uncomfortable clothes of excessive formality for the occasion, and the comic dramatist (and costume designer) insist on the exact punctilios of social ceremony, which have to be clearly defined before they are violated. The vain lady will, of course, be overdressed—too showy and too expensive for the occasion—and we will be struck by her vanity as soon as she comes on stage. The young lover and his sweetheart are usually inconspicuously dressed, neither too colorful nor too drab, because we are meant to concentrate on their sentiments and not to be sidetracked by their clothes. But folly of all sorts is exactly translated into its sartorial equivalent. Thus, Osric's plumed hat in *Hamlet*, which he keeps removing and putting on for the sake of some imagined deference, is an unforgettable detail of characterization.

Clothes are highly conventional in their significance, and fashions are very momentary and transitory. The mini/maxi controversy in the length of dresses and skirts, that raged so furiously in the 1960s, is now fortunately dead. Its implications are fading fast, and we will soon need footnotes and research bulletins of fashion institutes to remember what it was all about, but while it lasted it offered comic writers a way of making social points in a lucid and objective way. We can imagine Shaw's Major Barbara expressing her conversion to materialist values by switching from the maxi-granny-skirt of the Salvation Army uniform to a worldly micro-miniskirt of fawn-colored suede.

Modern dress, or some carefully articulated period dress, offer a director new perspectives on old plays. Joseph Papp's production of *Much Ado About Nothing* was exquisitely conceived in the dress, mores, and manners of the Spanish-American War. Sometimes these "translations" don't work and remain merely external and lifeless signs, but for comedy the costumes are a form of wit. The revival of *No, No, Nanette* owed much of its success to the persuasive nostalgia of its costumes and settings. Since character is so externally defined in comedy, the costumes provide the basis for specific and exact interpretations, which may also draw on the special associations of a bygone historical period. The Edwardian costuming of Shakespeare's comedies, which has become very popular, lends itself to a ready-made elegance and artificiality.

Disguise is an aspect of costume, since a character may change his identity by a mere change of dress. It is just as easy as that. The basic rule of the disguise convention, established in the plays of New Comedy, is simple: all disguise is good disguise and all disguise is impenetrable. No thorough transformations need be made, so that the audience can easily share the irony of one character's being in another character's clothes. Disguise offers a way of trying out wish-fulfillment roles. The king may disguise himself as a beggar in order to investigate what is really happening in his kingdom. Most commonly, a young lady in love disguises herself as a boy and enters the service of the very lord she is hopelessly in love with. Disguise allows the girl a freedom of expression she could not otherwise have, and she can play on the ironies of her transvestite apparel, or, to use the technical term, her crossdressing. In Elizabethan drama there was a further irony in the fact that all the female roles were played by boy actors. The easiness of disguise suits the mood of comedy, which delights in masquerading and make-believe and does not put a high value on the integral, unchanging personality. Disguise is a form of play, and it makes us aware of the illusions on which drama is based, since the actors themselves are always disguised as the characters they represent.

Comedy deals in public personalities and public faces. It is not subtlety we want but clarity, so that masks are often useful for comic characterization. The fixed expression is needed to define the type. The Italian Renaissance *commedia dell' arte* made extensive use of masks—not full masks, but partial ones that caricatured certain features, like the hooked nose and pointed chin of the *pantalone*, or old, avaricious fool, often a lawyer, and always grotesquely and desiccatedly in love with a beautiful, juicy, young girl. The white facial makeup of the clown is our best known surviving mask, which is painted directly on the skin, although the bulbous red nose is artificial. The clown is painted to look sad, and he looks sad whether he is laughing or crying—the fixed expression overrides any momentary contradictions. There is also the whiteface and the standardized black tights of the mime, most notably Marcel Marceau. His face is a nonhuman mask, an actor's face, expressionless and sad, and the emotions the mime arouses are simplified and exaggerated. We are meant to be acutely aware of the clown's separation from ordinary life and normal emotions. He is an adult imitating a child's directness and broadness of expression.

Comic characters begin with fixed and sometimes arbitrary values and connotations.

The art of comedy doesn't make any serious effort to conceal its artfulness or artificiality, and its highly conventional nature is an obvious reduction and simplification of human experience. We are not meant to argue with the assumptions of comedy. To say that they are not true to life seems to be saying nothing at all, since comedy is, in the Aristotelian sense, an "imitation" or mimesis of life and no substitute for the real thing. Comedy does not try to create lifelike characters, but pure and intense ones, who are not moderate, mixed, and fallible, but rather extremes, freaks, and caricatures of living persons.

The comic polarity of youth and age, for example, may be derived from real life, but it thrives in an atmosphere nourished by literary tradition. The relation of the comic idea to actual persons, young and old, is fortuitous, and neither proves nor disproves the validity of the comparison, as in the inimitable wording of the escape clause in the movies: "Any resemblance between the characters and persons living or dead is purely coincidental." By tradition, "youth and crabbed age cannot live together." They are natural antagonists, particularly because old men were once young men and every callow youth will eventually become the *senex* he so abhors. In Roman comedy the old father is jealous of his son for his sexual attraction and prowess, and the aged P may secretly be pursuing the same girl as the son. This creates complications. The old father's money gives him a natural advantage in the struggle, in which the son is deliberately impoverished and therefore powerless. But money is never enough, and the son triumphs over his obstructive father with the help of all those who favor young lovers rather than dried-up, impotent, and avaricious old men. "All those," of course, means virtually everybody, since who can refuse these irresistible propositions? The struggle seems to be heavily weighted against the son, whereas the comic odds are overwhelmingly set against the father. This is one illusion among many in the opposition between appearance and reality: solid, material obstacles give way immediately against the force of young love.

The comic assumptions have enormous romantic appeal, yet it would be difficult to argue that the old fathers are fairly represented. Where is their dignity and *gravitas?* Where is their warm and sentimental family feeling? The conventional types are caricatures, who are pitted against each other in predetermined scenarios, yet we are pleased to see avarice and lechery confuted and ardent passion celebrated. In *The Old Law* (1618), attributed to Middleton, Rowley, and Massinger, the son is much perturbed that his old father refuses to obey the new law, which calls upon all old persons to be put to death with grace and generosity—men at eighty and women at sixty—and so turn over their estates to their children. This may be a sardonic parody of a typical comic plot, but the son in the play is genuinely put out by the stubbornness and lawlessness of his old father, who insists on clinging to his miserable existence. Brabantio in *Othello* also fits the stereotype of the heavy father of comedy, as the theme of cuckoldry teeters on the edge of a traditional comic subject. Brabantio is badly served by the play, harried as he is by Iago on one side and his daughter Desdemona on the other. There is no possible resolution for his tragicomic difficulties, and he seems to die of a broken heart.

Little old ladies are not under the same handicaps as the fathers of comedy, and they lend themselves to more innocent amusement. The easiest thing to do is to reverse the cultural stereotypes. Put a machine gun in the lap of Whistler's Mother, or have her wistfully looking out into space at a blue movie, and you immediately have a comic situation, but maybe one that doesn't extend beyond a momentary glance at a cartoon. In *Arsenic and Old Lace*, the sweet old lady regularly poisons her gentlemen lodgers with elderberry wine, but manages never to alienate our feelings of warmth and sympathy. The little old ladies in tennis shoes who wreak havoc in their neighborhood in *Monty Python's Flying Circus* are characters in the same tradition. We don't expect to be mugged by some frail octogenarian in steel glasses, who hits us quick as a bunny with her weighted shopping bag, just as we don't expect blind people whom

Figure 5. Comic Mayhem: Mr. Muckle, The Blind Man (Charles Sellon), Destroying a Grocery Store, with W. C. Fields and Tammany Young Trying to Maintain Due Respect (*It's a Gift*, Paramount, 1934); *The Museum of Modern Art/Film Stills Archive.*

we are helping across the street to suddenly turn on us and offer grievous bodily harm.

We have been encouraged to think in stereotypes, which makes it possible for daring counter-stereotypes to be so effective. In W. C. Fields's movie *It's a Gift*, we watched with fascinated horror as Mr. Muckle, the blind man (played by Charles Sellon), laid waste an entire grocery store with his remarkable agile cane and purposive stomping. Beginning with a basket of eggs (see Figure 5), the destruction continued with calculated savagery until every last item in the store had been annihilated. We winced and laughed at this apocalyptic vision of the meek and helpless blind man taking his unanticipated revenge on the world of things.

In most comedies, wit replaces virtue and pretense is the greatest vice.

The morality of comedy is a favorite academic subject, and most comedies go out of their way to assure us that evil will be punished and good rewarded. What else is the happy ending, but a final reassurance that the good people have triumphed, and if the bad people are not severely chastized, that, too, is part of the good mood and desire for reconciliation with which comedy ends. But who are the good people and how is their virtue defined? The good people in comedy are usually the beautiful people, and not just in the Platonic sense, because everyone who is handsome, high-spirited, and young, who despises money (although he may need plenty of it), and who is charming, unpretentious, sociable, and generous tends to be rewarded in the end.

Virtue, in any of its stricter senses, gets very little play in comedy; it is definitely an embarrassing subject. Ben Jonson mercilessly satirizes his truth-speaking characters, who may, like Surly in *The Alchemist*, be so ill-willed, so mean-spirited, and so surly as to be incapable of appreciating the grand illusions of the alchemist's house. In the end, Surly is deprived of all the prizes he feels he has so strenuously won, including the rich, young, and yielding widow, Dame Pliant, and the symbolically named Lovewit takes all. Jonson and other comic writers are careful to pay lip service to morality, but wit outshines, outstrips, and outperforms goodness, and the comic action remains essentially amoral.

In this respect the comedy of the Restoration in England (from 1660 to roughly 1700) is not basically different from other comedy. Its subjects may be more risqué and it may neglect the expected moral tributes, but its amorality follows established comic usage. In Wycherley's *The Country Wife* (1675), Horner's outrageous report that he is impotent—meant to promote his sexual activity under the guise of a safe-conduct—comes directly out of Terence's comedy, *The Eunuch*. We don't see much of Horner's remarkable sex life, but we do hear a great deal about the hypocrisy of a society in which only appearances count. Horner is something like the satirical, malcontent railers of Elizabethan plays—Malevole in Marston's *The Malcontent*, or even Hamlet when he is inveighing against cosmetics and the false arts of women—rather than an unprincipled rake and insatiable lecher.

To be a rake is a fashionable posture for the comic hero. It means that he is unalterably opposed to the false worship of reputation and to all forms of hypocrisy and social pretense. He is the natural man, an admitted libertine, but also a man at liberty to speak his mind and to exercise an absolute freedom. The wits of Restoration comedy are always intelligent, lucid, and eloquent. They don't worry about virtue and vice, because the moral terms are themselves an expression of a hypocritical society. The only thing that matters is wit, which means free expression both in language and manners. In this way, wit replaces virtue as the criterion of value.

The greatest vice in comedy is hypocrisy, especially the preoccupation of polite society with appearances, which must be maintained at all costs. For the hypocrite, so long as the letter of the law is satisfied, it doesn't matter what consenting (and lecherous) adults do in private. This looks like an old-fashioned moral stance, but in practice the emphasis falls on pretense rather than full-flavored hypocrisy—on social rather than moral foibles. The pretended gentleman becomes the equivalent of the villain, and his labored and fatuous efforts to achieve distinction are automatically doomed to failure. Sir Fopling Flutter in *The Man of Mode* (1676) comes to mind, but his foolish concern with fancy dress—in all of its exact, fastidious detail, including the names of the actual establishments he frequents—has a certain innocent charm to it. Sir Fopling deflects any righteous indignation, as do other pretenders to wit and fashion.

In *The Country Wife*, the foolish suitor of Alithea—whose name means "truth," and who is, almost for that reason alone, a dull and disappointing character—practically invites the gallants to sleep with his wife-to-be. This pretense at aristocratic nonchalance is, of course, a superb piece of folly that cannot go unpunished. Pretenders of any sort are the proper targets of the wits, including false critics, tellers of bad jokes, and poetasters. In a triumph of the aesthetic sensibility, Mirabell and Millamant in *The Way of the World* (1700) show that they are ideally suited for each other by being able to complete each other's couplets. The couplets, like some harrowing but unknown test by which the mythological hero proves his fitness, seal the marriage of true minds and true wits.

The witty, clever, and ingenious slave of Roman comedy may be related to the witty, dashing, and satirical rake of Restoration comedy. Both function completely outside conventional morality and their wit replaces any moral claims. They are energetic, forceful, and colorful figures, audacious in intrigue, brilliant psychologists and manipulators of men, but never offensive, self-righteous, or in any way self-important. In other words, they are motivated by the spirit of fun and games and not by the lure of any real or imagined material rewards. The prizes they may gather at the end are always made to seem gratuitous, and their attitude is one of studied casualness. Pseudolus in Plautus's farce boasts about how easy his impossible task will be, and he has the effrontery to warn his victims that he will cheat them—and even to place bets with them about the outcome. The point, of course, is that the comic slave has the true aristocratic manner. He is purposefully insolent, while his master has a servile, petty, and gross outlook, without the slightest trace of imagination. The slave must occasionally play humble to prevent the savage beatings that are threatened, but the perils add zest to the game, and no one seriously believes that the slave will be punished. It is up to him to figure out how, although a slave, he can nevertheless be a winner.

The social implications of the witty slave (or comic servant) are sometimes suggested by the playwright (or self-consciously intruded, as in the case of Beaumarchais' Figaro or Stoppard's Bennett in *Travesties*), but this significance is not relevant to the comic action. The slave is not a cunning revolutionary teasing his master with a show of force (or farce); rather, his lack of status stimulates his comic invention. Since he has no stake in society, he has absolutely nothing to lose, and he can therefore give his imagination free rein. Both the witty slave and the young libertine are disinterested figures. They have been relieved of the burden of responsibility, of maintaining their reputation, and even of gainful employment. They are uniquely in a position to be free men.

Pretenders are not only deflated in comedy but also displayed and celebrated.

The purging of antisocial impulses and eccentric preoccupations at the end of a play raises a problem. We have grown fond of our humorous characters, their nuttiness endears them to us, and, to tell the truth, their quirks and their whimsies are their only distinctive traits. Put them out of their humors and they are only ordinary, drab mortals, but in the full flush of their madness they have a certain brilliance. The ending of comedy, especially comedy of humors, tends to be deflationary, as the various pretenders are assessed at their true value and put in their place—put down, as we would say. So there is a danger in insisting too strictly on judgment (as Jonson does in *Volpone*), because the comic effect may be hampered, or at least neutralized.

In comedy we cling to illusions even when we know they are wrong, not only cling to them but actively pursue them against our own better judgment. Truth and morality are suspended as we watch the fascinating spectacle of con men magnificently conning us. The justification is in the magnificence. All the memorable comic pretenders are great talkers: inventive, hyperbolic, grandly absurd. They are superlatives after their own kind, nonpareils, extraordinary men. If the purging of humors is comic therapy, then we might well prefer the sickness to the cure. We would like to believe that the pretenders merely suffer temporary setbacks and will emerge again in full flower.

No matter how brilliant his successes, Charlie Chaplin always managed to lose all and to end his movies as the tramp, without the girl who regarded him so pantingly, without the riches he had accidentally acquired, and without the exalted position in the world that had come to him by pure chance. Comfortably stripped of all wordly encumbrances except the packet suspended over his shoulder by his cane, he walked tranquilly down the road and into the horizon to encounter new adventures and new successes. The pretense of wordly success was innocent, if not giddy, an effect of high spirits, and no permanent claims on reality were intended. Comic metaphysics postulates life as a gambling casino, in which one wins or loses with equal facility and equal unconcern, since money itself is unreal.

The military pretender to heroic feats (who is actually a coward) is one of the most permanent of comic types. Plautus's *Miles Gloriosus* displays the character in fully developed form: Pyrgopolynices is a ferocious figure; he has the stature and the manner of a soldier, with all the appropriate phrases and gestures; he dresses magnificently and plays the part with distinction; he is inordinately boastful, with a circumstantial detail hard to resist, and, in fact, the *miles gloriosus* (or glorified soldier) is usually called the "braggart." To say that he is also an abject coward seems to be an extraneous admission, like the fact that he may be growing bald. It seems to have nothing to do with the perfect figure of a soldier we see before us, who is obviously the "real thing." There is a certain vague embarrassment in admitting to cowardice, but it seems to enter only as a side point, as Casanova might be forced to confess that, although he is impotent, this minor impediment can't affect his performance as a lover. It is absurd, but deliciously so, and we must finally accept Pyrgopolynices as the actor of a brave man (which he actually is) rather than the brave man himself. We are made to feel that it would be vulgar to be merely a soldier, and a courageous one at that. To play the *part* of a soldier is what is essential, not to *be* a soldier.

Jonson's Captain Bobadill in *Every Man in His Humor* impersonates a veteran of the wars and a fearful swaggerer with great dignity and great success. He insists on all the punctilios of honor, and he is a master of the duelling code as well as the instruction manuals on the art of handling rapier and dagger. He approaches violence with a thoughtfulness that is admirable; he controls himself, he offers excuses, he tries to mitigate aggression for fear of the dire consequences. That he is also the grossest of cowards hardly seems to matter. It becomes buried, as it were, or concealed under the magnificence of his eloquence and wit. The elaborateness of his boasting assures us that he is a coward from the first moment, so that there is no sudden, deflationary effect. We are not meant to be taken by surprise. Captain Bobadill is a *miles gloriosus* pure and simple, just as other men are carpenters, bricklayers, statesmen, and even soldiers, and, as Falstaff says, " 'Tis no sin for a man to labor in his vocation" (*Henry IV, Part 1* 1.2.108–9).

Falstaff is, of course, the most splendid *miles gloriosus* of the comic tradition. Although he cannot be so easily characterized as the purer types, he retains one essential feature: he is a great talker and a great actor. He is never an abject figure, but always maintains his dignity and resourcefulness. He may not be able to defend himself physically, but he is never at a loss for words. Falstaff is vital to the composition of a military and heroic play, whose high ideal of honor also involves butchery, treachery, and meaningless slaughter. Hotspur turns out to be an almost guileless victim of his own high-sounding words, and the "grinning honor" of the dead Sir Walter Blunt is plainly ironic. Falstaff is an entertainer and a comic philosopher, out of place on the field of battle, yet an indispensable spokesman for the life values. He is never really unmasked, as Parolles is in *All's Well That Ends Well*, since his claims were never taken seriously at any point in the play.

The presence of Pistol in *Henry IV, Part 2* and in *Henry V* gives the swaggering action an exceptionally literary flavor. Pistol is a purely imaginative creation, whose discourse is composed almost entirely from scraps of old plays, especially garbled heroic scraps like:

> *These be good humors, indeed! Shall packhorses*
> *And hollow pampered jades of Asia,*

> *Which cannot go but thirty mile a day,*
> *Compare with Caesars, and with Cannibals [Hannibals],*
> *And Trojan Greeks? Nay, rather damn them with*
> *King Cerberus, and let the welkin [sky] roar. (Henry IV,*
> *   Part 2 2.4.167–72)*

Pistol's pretense needs no comic purgation to restore the social equilibrium. We need more of it, not less. Why seek to extinguish so inimitable a voice? Pistol frightens no one and is hardly part of that larger body of England that Prince Hal is trying so valiantly to protect from the evil designs of traitors. Without properly acknowledging it, Hal needs Falstaff, Pistol, and their crew in his regime. It is a mark of the narrow exclusiveness of the new society—surely a sign of failure in the recently crowned King—that he has to banish them.

Pedants are pretenders of a different sort, but pretenders nevertheless. They lay claim to a vast body of learning, usually in Latin and Greek, and act as the high priests of arcane knowledge not immediately available to ordinary men. Their superiority is attested by their subject, of which they act as the keepers, the proprietors, the interpreters to a philistine and materialistic world. The pedant is a school teacher, usually a grammar-school teacher, who is accustomed to dealing with children, so that his lofty condescension and tyrannical pettiness are professional deformations of his calling. Above all, the pedant is very knowing, full of the self-important ironies of an in-group, which looks with pity on the rudeness and barbarism of the rest of the world. The pedant's vanity is innocent and part of his charm. He is a true naïf in his firm conviction that all men are foolish except himself; this is the seed of his madness.

In reality, the pedant knows nothing except the forms and rules and technicalities of things, especially of language. His mind is so filled with the burden of conjugations, declensions, and the vagaries of irregular verbs that there is no room left for anything else. He is a living grammar book, a walking dictionary, and a compendium of useless, pointless, and totally irrelevant knowledge. Holofernes, the inimitable pedant of *Love's Labor's Lost*, and his cronies "have been at a great feast of languages and stol'n the scraps" (5.1.39–40). He can scarcely utter a single sentence that is not pedantically self-conscious and self-regarding, as if his expressions were themselves taken from elementary language manuals.

This is the source of Ionesco's brilliant farce, *The Bald Soprano*, whose profound inanities are actually sample sentences from the Assimil conversation course for English. The implications of this dazzling pastiche of language instruction are developed in Ionesco's *The Lesson*, which features a homicidal pedant discoursing with frenzied intensity on the fine points of Neo-Spanish linguistics. As it turns out, the forms of Neo-Spanish are identical with those in "Austrian and Neo-Austrian or Hapsburgian, as well as the Esperanto, Helvetian, Monacan, Swiss, Andorran, Basque, and jai alai groups. . . . ," all of which abstruse knowledge the young pupil must absorb in her valiant attempt at the "total doctorate." As the Maid warns the Professor, knowing full well where all this pedantry will end: "Philology leads to calamity!"

Pedants are not limited to teachers, but may include any character preoccupied with the jargon and technicalities of a profession to the exclusion of its substance. Legal pedantry is a frequent source of humor in Renaissance comedy, since "law French" and "law Latin" are highly specialized languages with no relation to ordinary, living speech. The comic rule is: the more abstract, the more mummified, the better. The lawyers (or their clerks) display their erudition to establish their superiority to their clients and also to lay the basis for high fees. Their legal incantations are sometimes pig-Latin translations of ordinary, foolish discourse, but the sound is right and a proper atmosphere of dignity is established.

In Jonson's *Epicoene*, Cutbeard, the barber, in his mock role as canon lawyer, assaults Morose, the man who can stand no noise, with the twelve bases for annulment: "But there are duodecim impedimenta, twelve impediments as we call 'em, all which do not 'dirimere contractum,' but 'irritum reddere matrimonium,' as we say in the canon law, not take away the bond, but cause a nullity therein." Notice how self-importantly Cutbeard uses "we" for his learned in-group—there is nothing personal in what he is saying—and how patiently he translates the Latin for his ignorant auditors. To the man who cannot tolerate noise, the legal words assault him with thunderous force, and the use of Latin endows the proceeding with a false sense of gravity and importance. This kind of discourse, full of incomprehensible but threatening accusations and stipulations, is itself a form of aggression both in sound and in substance. Morose is caught in the toils of the law—not even that, but merely in the words of the law (or, more exactly, in the sound of those words), but words and realities merge and are equally threatening.

Machiavelli's *Mandragola* uses mock-medical language in much the same way, and doctors, as Molière so well demonstrated, play an analogous role to lawyers in the history of comedy. They are both self-important impostors. The pedantry is usually pure pretense, but it makes for a wonderfully inflated discourse. In one scene in *Mandragola*, Callimaco, the young lover pretending to be a physician, examines the beautiful Lucrezia's urine specimen and comments learnedly on it: *"Nam mulieris urinae sunt semper maioris glossitiei et albedinis et minoris pulchritudinis quam virorum"* ("For the urines of women are always more glossy and whitish and less beautiful than those of men"). Messer Nicia, the husband, is much impressed by Latin, no matter how foolish, and he becomes an easy dupe and accomplice in the sexual assault on his wife. He is subdued not only by Latin, but by his own groveling self-conceit and toadyism; he dotes on authority.

In Molière the physicians are all, without exception, quacks who prey on the needs of a credulous society. The larger point is that the society idolizes impostors while rejecting simple, honest men, who refuse to produce the marks and tokens and signs of respectable professionalism. In *The Doctor in Spite of Himself (Le Médecin Malgré Lui*, 1666), it is remarkably easy for Sganarelle to impersonate a physician. All he needs to do is to speak a gibberish of meaningless Latin, mostly taken from an elementary grammar book: *"Cabricias, arci thuram, catalamus, singulariter, nominativo, haec musa, la muse, bonus, bona, bonum. Deus sanctus, est-ne oratio latinas? Etiam, oui. Quare? pourquoi? Quia substantivo, et adjectivum, concordat in generi, numerum, et casus."* As the stage direction indicates, Sganarelle speaks *"avec enthousiasme,"* delighting in his medical triumph. The entire passage won't be translated here—most of it is nonsense—but the last sentence is the old grammatical maxim: "Because the substantive and the adjective agree in gender, number, and case." The words don't actually matter, and one Latin phrase is as good as any other to confer medical dignity on the speaker.

This is a celebration of pedantry, according to the formalist principles enunciated by the conclave of physicians in Act II, Scene iii, of *Love, the Doctor* (*L'Amour Médecin*, 1665): "A dead man is only a dead man and is of no consequence, but a formality neglected carries a notable stigma against the whole body of doctors." Which worthy pronouncement leads inevitably to the moral imperative of M. Bahis: "It is better to die according to the rules than to escape with your life by not following the rules" (II, v). Better for whom? Clearly for the doctors who remain alive. This makes a sharp distinction between the conservative and the radical temperament, and for Molière's ridiculous doctors, forms, rules, procedures, formalities—ultimately language—is the only reality.

Religious fanatics and enthusiasts of all kinds are also pedants in their own way, especially in their narrow and literal insistence on their own tenets to the exclusion of all other truths. Puritans, particularly, were mercilessly (but unforgettably) satirized by Ben Jonson and others for their self-regarding, over-weening militancy. They are the modern-day Pharisees, the great proponents of the letter of the law—and it is noteworthy how often their rigid, Old Testament religion is referred to simply as the "law." The dramatists' hatred of the Puritans (who, in their turn, violently attacked the institution of plays and theater) endowed their portraits of Puritans with vitality and vigor.

Jonson's Zeal-of-the-land Busy in *Bartholomew Fair* speaks with an extraordinary energy. On the question of eating pork at the Fair, he reasons with persuasive casuistry:

> It may be eaten, and in the Fair, I take it, in a booth, the
> tents of the wicked. The place is not much, not very
> much; we may be religious in midst of the profane, so it be
> eaten with a reformed mouth, with sobriety, and
> humbleness; not gorged in with gluttony or greediness;
> there's the fear: for, should she [the pregnant Win-the-
> fight Littlewit, who longs to eat pig] go there, as taking
> pride in the place, or delight in the unclean dressing, to
> feed the vanity of the eye or the lust of the palate, it were
> not well, it were not fit, it were abominable, and not good.
> (1.6.66–74)

It is remarkable how deeply Jonson must have immersed himself in Puritan rhetoric in order to write this passage, which is brilliant both for itself and as parody.

The point of the passage is abundantly clear: Rabbi Busy is a pious humbug and a fraud. His religious zeal is entirely a matter of words, but what magnificent and unforgettable words! We are back at the comic paradox with which we began. The pretenders must finally be exposed and deflated, but what splendid entertainment to listen to them talk and to observe their beautiful professionalism. Whatever Jonson's private views about Puritans—and we know that he despised them—there is no denying that Zeal-of-the-land Busy is grandly shown off in *Bartholomew Fair*. He is one of Jonson's most successful comic creations.

Comedy deals not with representative types, but with extremes and caricatures.

Aristotle's ideal man in the *Nicomachean Ethics*, who finds happiness and peace of mind by seeking his comfortable niche in the mean between extremes, has little place in comedy. The art of comedy is typically concerned not with the normal man, but with persons who cultivate the extremes—either excess or defect, too much or too little; it doesn't matter so long as the efforts are out of proportion, disharmonious, and incongruous. The types in comedy are not realistic portraits of average men in everyday situations. This is the point at which a good deal of domestic comedy on television begins, but once the intrigue plot gets moving, these ordinary people are soon catapulted into extraordinary complications, bizarre misunderstandings, freak accidents, unbelievable coincidences, and a peep into the possibilities of chaos and mayhem from which they recoil in simulated horror.

Norman Lear's *All in the Family* shows us a normal, decent, hard-working, right-thinking American family only at the beginning and the end of the show, when the values of the sponsor and his consuming audience are vociferously asserted. In the projection and development of the adventures that befall Archie Bunker and his typical American family, we are cut adrift from any reassuring normalities. The characters may be representative types because they are a cross section of American family life, but what happens to them is not representative at all, in the sense that the Lynds's sociological survey of the mythical Middletown, U.S.A., shows life as it was actually lived in the 1920s and 1930s. The "realism" of *All in the Family* is riddled with the wild, wish-fulfillment fantasies of comedy. Otherwise, why would the program be so successful, spinning off minor characters into their own independent series?

Ethnic humor offers a case in point about whether comedy deals with national character norms or with extremes and caricatures that are artfully attached to popular stereotypes. Jokes about national types really have little or nothing to do with the groups to which they are connected. They rely on traditional formulas, which can be applied to whatever national group happens to be in fashion or out of fashion in a particular place at any particular moment. The following question and answer joke can be adapted to any two nationalities favored by the speaker: "What is the difference between an Irishman and a Pole pissing in the sink? The Irishman takes the dishes out first." Usually ethnic jokes seize on some cultural trait attributed to the subject group: the formality of Englishmen, the heaviness and drunkenness of Germans, the French instinct for sophisticated sex, the clever and ambitious practicality of Jews, the sentimental and maudlin attachment of Irishmen to home and country. But these attributes are actually vague and ill-defined and can easily be shifted about for the occasion. The Jewish jokes Jews tell among themselves are different from the Jewish jokes current in middle America, which may be tinged with anti-semitic assumptions. And the same goes for Armenian jokes and minstrel-show darkie jokes complete with Negro spiritual accents.

Ethnic jokes can generally be told with interchangeable nationalities. For example, "How can you identify the groom at a Polish wedding? He's the one in the clean bowling shirt" echoes an old formula: "How can you identify the best man at a nudist wedding?" The bride might well be Rumanian in the following exchange: "How can you identify the bride at a Polish wedding? She's the one in the cute maternity dress." A final example in the question-answer form has a mock authenticity, because it plays on the grossest of cultural stereotypes: "What's the right career for the son of a Polish-Jewish marriage? Janitor in a medical school." The joke is a caricature of the upward mobility of Jews crossed with the downward mobility of Poles. With a few changes it could be translated into any other pair of antithetic nationalities favored by the speaker (Japanese-Korean, Swedish-Finnish, etc.).

In the typical ethnic joke, the ethnic characteristics are supplied by the teller according to his own sense of his audience. There is a story about two Germans driving on the New Jersey Turnpike, who suddenly see a fat pig on the side of the road and rush out to put it in their car. (Why two Germans? Why four Hawaiians in Joe Cook's book, *Why I Will Not Imitate Four Hawaiians?*) As the two Germans with the pig in their car approach the toll booth at the Lincoln Tunnel, they begin to get nervous. They decide to put a shawl around the pig's head and to sit it upright in the front seat with them, so that, if they go through quickly enough, the toll collector will think it's a woman. To their great surprise, they manage to get through the tollbooth without any hassle, but just as they are driving into the tunnel, one toll-collector says to the other: "Hey, did you see that?" "Yeah," says the other knowingly, and the first snaps back with moral indignation: "What's a nice Polish girl like that doing with a couple of Germans?" This joke lends itself to other ethnic pairings, either more or less inflammatory in the immediate context.

The following Italian joke has nothing particularly Italian about it except the accent, which comes from the dialect spoken by Chico Marx. The joke is given in shortened form, purely, as Freud says in his book on jokes, for purposes of illustration and analysis: A young man comes back from college during a vacation and enjoys the warmth and hospitality of his home. After an especially plentiful and tasty dinner, he tells his mother that he wishes to have a serious talk with her. "Mom," he begins, "I just met the most wonderful and beautiful girl, we fell in love immediately, and we want to get married." The mother is absolutely taken aback and on the point of an emotional crisis. She pleads with her son to reconsider his hasty decision. "Ain't I bin a gudda mudder to you, bambino? Doan I givva you lasagna, manicotti, spaghetti, antipasto? Why you wanna doa dis to me? You no luvva me?" The son is getting extremely wrought up and he cuts his mother short: "Mom, you

"I can't swim! Would ten dollars help?"

Figure 6. Comic Irrelevance (Handelsman in *The New Yorker*, July 17, 1971; *reprinted by permission of* The New Yorker).

can't speak to me like this." The mother replies, with passion: "Why canna I speaka dissa way to you? Ain't youa me bambino? Ain't I you mudder?" The son answers with finality: "Mom, you can't speak to me like this because you're not Italian."

This is really a shaggy-dog story, which transfers its anticlimax to the ethnic mode in order to freshen up the situation, but the indulgent reader will agree that the story could use any recognizable national accent with equal success or failure. There are undoubtedly national differences in humor, and jokes certainly carry strong cultural connotations, but the ethnic stereotypes we have been talking about are perpetuated by the media rather than by ethnics themselves on the streets of a typical American city.

Extremes generate laughter, especially when presented in opposing pairs of the Mutt and Jeff variety. The country bumpkin or rube is in classic opposition to the city slicker, and the foolish naivety of one stimulates the preposterous sophistication of the other. The confrontation is a set up, in which naive questions can be absurdly posed and answered. Wycherley's country wife (in *The Country Wife*) wants to know what the harm is in kissing, and all the London gallants rush in to instruct her. On the other side, there is *The New Yorker* cartoon by Handelsman, showing an urbane gentleman with hat, glasses, and bowtie at the end of a pier, looking with some consternation at a drowning man and asking nervously: "I can't swim! Would ten dollars help?" (see Figure 6). In an early Mickey Mouse animated cartoon, the citified Mickey is puzzled about how to milk a cow until he discovers that he can bend the tail in the shape of a crank. The exceedingly passive man may be paired with an excessively active one, as in certain straightman-interlocutor dialogues, where the extreme slowness and stupidity of the inactive partner is highlighted by the sharpness and quickness of the other. If the pair is in good working order, the humor will presumably come from both sides, which activate each other like a teetering seesaw.

The negative part of the equation is generally more interesting than the positive. Thus the absence of any activity at all has a fascination greater than frenzied activity, which is, in any case, difficult to sustain. There is a story told by I. A. Richards, the critic-philosopher-poet and inventor of Basic English, about a philosopher in China lecturing on Mencius on a particularly warm and fly-filled day and falling asleep in the middle of a sentence. The words of the sentence gradually became fewer and fewer and more widely spaced until they ceased altogether. But how could one be sure that the sleep was not just an exceptionally long pause between words rather than the discrete end of something? One can imagine this story being performed by a gifted mime.

Many of Beckett's characters seem to resemble this philosopher, as their speech breaks down and parts of their body mysteriously disappear. There is a boredom so intense that it becomes fascinating, and the bore achieves stature as a demonic comic genius. Is he really a bore, or is he merely playing the role of a bore with consummate artistry? It's teasing to speculate on a boredom so pure and so excruciating that it creates its own self-immolation—a phoenix and an apotheosis of boredom. With one more turn of the screw, we are suddenly freed from material preoccupations and purged of organic discomfort as we pass from pain to pleasure. At such extremes, laughter is an expression of physical release and spiritual liberation. It is a nice paradox to believe that comedy not only deals in extremes, but that these extremes are also subtly connected with each other and that the free spirit will know how to move effortlessly from one extreme to the other.

III

The Structure of Comedy

The art of comedy is highly patterned. Comedies begin with type characters and traditionally comic situations and develop these characters and situations in unconventional and sometimes wild and frenzied ways. Novelty is not sought for its own sake, but rather as a variation on old themes. It may well be that a joke can neither be created nor destroyed and that every possible joke is a new twist on an already existing formula. There is something comforting about old jokes and old plots. These fixed comic structures and established principles of comic development are not a liability but something inherently attractive. Although the ability to tell jokes and to write comedies may be a natural gift that cannot be either learned or taught, the art of comedy may still be profitably studied. It has a central body of doctrines and practices from which, if we can't train ourselves how to be funny, we can at least learn when to laugh. We can also develop our feeling for how the action in comedy is moving—what we may call our comic sense of direction. In this context, comic structure may be defined as a set of complex anticipations on the part of the audience.

Comic structure also depends upon a prevailingly optimistic tone. If there are difficulties and obstacles, we have deep assurance that they are only temporary and fortuitous. There is no tragic coloring or tragic metaphysics, which insists that "something is rotten in the state of Denmark" or that "Fair is foul and foul is fair." We have no ancient curse on the house, as in Greek tragedy, and no dark oracle hanging over the action and pushing the characters to purposed and fateful ends. We have faith in the comic structure. We know that, despite all appearances to the contrary, the plot will and *must* generate the preordained happy ending. There is a sense of inevitability in the way that comedy produces comedy. In other words, once you begin with a set of comic propositions or comic intrigue, you are safely secured in the world of comedy, in which the comic resolution will fulfill our original expectations.

Comedies usually begin with a startling pronouncement or an outrageous situation.

To begin with a startling pronouncement or an outrageous situation provides the initial jerk or impetus for the action. As audience, we start with the noose about our necks and the playwright or jokester gives it a little jerk just to remind us to pay attention. Curiously enough, comedies often begin with some climactic event, which may be more dire—or at least more convincing—than the actual climax of the work, especially since comic climaxes tend to be extremely melodramatic and implausible. We have some outrageous, arbitrary edict: all Syracusans discovered in Ephesus will be immediately put to death (as in Shakespeare's *The Comedy of Errors*). The reasons for this cruel law are left vague and unexplained, but, as good comic auditors, we accept what we are told without passing judgment. Comedy literally demands the willing suspension of disbelief, but, unlike tragedy, the audience is never supposed to empathize with the characters and to lose itself in the suspension. We are expected to remain aware of the arbitrary nature of our act and to remember that our suspension of disbelief is a temporary and voluntary agreement for purposes of the fiction.

The initial jerk of the comic cord is meant to shock us. How many jokes begin with some startling pronouncement: A man swallows his glass eye and goes to the doctor for advice; A bartender is swinging his parrot on a green silk cord, when one of his customers suddenly asks, "Why are you doing that?"; A man with a terrible stammer (or harelip) applies for a job as a radio announcer and the interviewer wants to know if he is Jewish. Where do we go from here? A collection of first lines of jokes, carefully indexed, would be an extremely valuable contribution to the art of comedy and would serve the same function as a pianist's fake-book, which collects snatches of melodies and chords to stimulate the memory. Beginnings of jokes (and of comedies) are felt to be so distinctive because they plunge us immediately into the world of comic artifice. We cannot properly begin with the punch line or the dénouement, but even if we do, we are exercising a deliberate irony, which only has meaning as a reversal of conventional expectations. Perhaps "one-liners"—like Henny Youngman's "I'm sixty-six and it takes me all night to do what I used to do all night"—make such successful jokes because there is only one single burst, like a punch line, and we don't have to grapple with any narrative structure.

In the example of the outrageous edict from *The Comedy of Errors*, death is threatened to all Syracusan interlopers in Ephesus, and poor Aegeon, looking for his lost twin son, is immediately swept up in the net of the law. His death hangs over the entire play, and yet it is wrong to think of the comedy as having tragicomic overtones. Death is unreal, it is merely a plot device, and the institution of law—much favored as a comic subject—does not enunciate immutable truths. Like the plot of comedy, the law is flexible, much influenced by circumstances (and bribes), subject to bizarre and brilliant interpretations (as that of the pound of flesh by Portia in *The Merchant of Venice*), and always a plaything of chance and fortune. In comedy, human considerations always triumph over law, so that any insistence on the letter of the law, like Shylock's harping on his bond, is doomed to failure. The comic spirit is meant to prevail over mere technicalities, but the technicalities are usually invoked at the beginning of a comedy to provide the obstacles that must eventually be overcome. These barriers are essential for the comic structure, whose progress resembles an obstacle course. The winner must prove himself worthy of the prizes he is sure to receive at the end: the beautiful bride, the pot of gold, powerful connections, a place in the new regime, and a big house with compactor, microwave oven, and self-opening garage.

Medicine is another technical and autonomous system that functions like law in the history of comedy. How many jokes begin with a man visiting his doctor, or, more fashionably, his psychoanalyst? Lawyers and doctors are mysterious experts, gurus and shamans upon whose decisions our lives and fortunes depend. In a secular age, we approach them with the awe once reserved for priests. Our attitude encourages our own victimization, so that we are usually self-defeated and self-destroyed—casualties of comic justice. We seem to be searching for the truth, but we are actually only pursuing our own vanity.

Jonson's *Volpone* (1606) has such universal appeal because its action turns so significantly on greed. Volpone and his accomplice, Mosca, are busily engaged in the *captatio* swindle, in which the "dying" invalid is trying to choose his heir. The play abounds in medical expertise, as the status of the dying man's health becomes a matter of intense competition and speculation. When he is not playing dead, or near-dead, Volpone engages in medical practice as Scoto the Magnificent, who extols the virtues of his medicine in the public square: ". . . a most sovereign and approved remedy: the *mal caduco*, cramps, convulsions, paralyses, epilepsies, *tremor cordia*, retired nerves, ill vapours of the spleen, stoppings of the liver, the stone, the strangury, *hernia ventosa, iliaca passio;* stops a *dysenteria* immediately; easeth the torsion of the small guts; and cures *melancholia hypocondriaca*, being taken and applied according to my printed receipt" (2.2.102–9). The torrent of medical jargon is meant to impress us, and, specifically, to help seduce Celia, the young and beautiful wife of the foolish Corvino.

Comedy needs all the obstacles, obstructions, bars, barriers, lets, and hindrances it can invent in order to get moving—the more the merrier, on the principle that the greater the initial difficulties, the sweeter will be the resolution. The dénouement in comedy is literally an untying of knots, and plot complications are emphasized for the delight of the audience. In the original shaggy-dog story, there is in fact no resolution at all. The point of it is that it has no point, and the meandering circumstances, specifications, and involvements are indulged purely for their own sake. It is hardly even anticlimactic, since no climax, no matter how thunderous, could possibly satisfy our inflamed expectations. It is a dimensionless story, and whether the dog is ultimately too shaggy or not shaggy enough (as in competing versions) ceases to be important.

Comedy is committed to plot in a way that tragedy isn't, and comedy is also committed to the idea of magical transformations and metamorphoses. The best tragedies, like the Oedipus story, are extremely simple, so that the real affinities of comedy are with melodrama rather than tragedy. Both are heavily plotted—extremely artificial, we might say, as opposed to natural, believable sequences of events—and melodrama may actually be a kind of reversed comedy (or tragicomedy), since it always has a happy ending, no matter how sentimental. Melodrama lends itself extremely well to parody, and it is sometimes difficult to determine whether it is intended to be taken literally or parodistically. In any case, it really doesn't matter, since the audience may delight in feeling superior to a temperance farce like *Ten Nights in a Barroom*, whose ostensible purpose it finds ridiculous.

Lysander's observation in *A Midsummer Night's Dream*, "The course of true love never did run smooth" (1.1.134), is more or less the prescribed formula for love comedies. True love *must* be difficult in order to be worthy of its practitioners. *Nil sine labore magno* ("nothing without great effort") and *finis coronat opus* ("the end crowns the work"). So the playwright sets about blearing the eyes of the lovers and putting booby traps in their path. Complex erotic psychology is simplified in order to work out the set equations, and the doctrine of love at first sight proves to be extremely useful to the dramatist to get the plot underway. It's hard to believe that anyone seriously credited this notion as an account of human behavior, but of course it's sex rather than love that the comic dramatist is talking about. As Zeffirelli's movie clearly brought home to adolescent audiences, once Romeo and Juliet are *in* love with each other, they burn to *make* love with each other, and the play remains a comedy for a remarkably long time, or at least refuses to disclose its tragic potential.

Machiavelli's *Mandragola* (about 1518) is more purely a wish-fulfillment comedy, but once Callimaco, the young lover, reveals the alarming fact that he must sleep with Lucrezia (the beautiful wife of Messer Nicia, an aging and thoroughly stupid lawyer), or die, his remarkable wish is not so easily gratified. Notice how reverently wishes are respected in comedy, the more outrageous the wish the better. No one has the audacity to tell the male lead that he is a lustful brute—that would be embarrassing and inappropriate, and who in the play has sufficient moral stamina to make such a pronouncement?—but only problems of management and organization are considered. How to go about it? Once the audience faces up to the sensual nature of most love comedy, it can better appreciate the obstacles that are introduced to make the rewards more delicious. Nowhere do the difficulties seem more overwhelming than at the very beginning, before the plot to minimize and overcome those difficulties gets started. The comic plot is, in some sense, a rational structure created to explain away the obstacles. But before the process begins in earnest, we must experience that feeling of dire climax and catastrophe with which many comedies begin. To pursue the medical metaphor, the comic plot is meant to purge us of our initial anxieties and to relieve us of our tensions and fears.

In comedy (as in other extreme situations), money helps. The general rule is that comic characters are not supposed to refuse money graciously offered, except if their social aloofness or impregnable integrity has been clearly established from the start. Money is a radical test of the reality principle, and its numerical character lends itself to large and obvious distinctions. The rich and available widow, played by Margaret Dumont in many Marx Brothers' movies (see Figure 7), has both dimension and money, so that her ex-

Figure 7. Comic Nonchalance: Groucho Marx and Margaret Dumont in *The Cocoanuts* (Paramount, 1929); *The Museum of Modern Art / Film Stills Archive.*

pensive pearls are shown to advantage throughout the ballroom, as if from a colossal statue. She is the center of attention, and all eyes are literally on her (and her expansive and well decorated bosom).

Even Shakespeare is not so blinded by his romantic plots to neglect the hard fact that the love pursuit is often begun for money—to repair one's mysteriously damaged fortunes, as Petruchio pur-

sues Kate in *The Taming of the Shrew*—but may end in real affection, as with Bassanio and Portia in *The Merchant of Venice*. In that
play, Shylock may not be so deranged to be crying "My ducats and
my daughter" (2.8.17), since Lorenzo would not settle for less than
Jessica *and* her father's jewels and money. Some of the most poignant lines in the play relate to the turquoise ring given to Shylock
by his deceased wife, Leah, which his foolish daughter and
Lorenzo have bartered for a monkey. It is a ring that Shylock himself would not have traded "for a wilderness of monkeys"
(3.1.115–16).

Young lovers insist on sex and money, and older lovers always
demand at least money, so that the love plot becomes a showcase
for the values of an acquisitive society. Perhaps we could describe
comic plots as mechanisms of acquisition. Something is always
being sought, pursued, hunted, bargained for, or stolen—
something of value, be it love, sex, or money. The plot begins with
an announcement of the stakes and an account of the limiting con-
ditions and attendant difficulties. The action then moves inexorably to the overcoming of these difficulties and the triumphant acquisition of the prize.

The comic action is developed by repetition, accumulation, and snowballing.

Repetition may be the single most important mechanism in comedy. In a play, repetition is essential to develop the original dilemma or plot complication. The world of comedy is simple, perhaps even simplified, and complex motivation and subtle
psychology are reduced to a working model that everyone can understand. Difficulties are smoothed over, or at least redefined into
practical formulas that may not apply to real life, but are admirably
suited to the oppositions and balances of comedy. If life is a game,
then in most comedies the players on either side are clearly iden-
tified, the rules are few and succinct, and the action consists of a
series of encounters and skirmishes in which friend and foe are
plainly distinguishable. Tragedy, as distinct from melodrama, is

played by different rules, and friend and foe may be obscured by metaphysical ambiguities—the protagonist may be his own worst enemy, as in the case of Macbeth, Oedipus, and others. It's hard to imagine the comic protagonist as his own worst enemy, since he depends so absolutely on his own wit and wits for survival. He may give the impression of a determined course of self-destruction, but this is only an ironic disguise for vigorously self-indulgent and self-protective behavior.

There may be a strongly neurological basis for repetition. We need more research on a physiological theory of laughter and comedy, which hasn't advanced much beyond Charles Darwin's impressive chapter in *The Expression of the Emotions in Man and Animals* (1872). Repetition, especially of a gesture or expression, arouses strong feelings of expectation, so that any part of the original gesture or expression may be sufficient to produce the original reaction, by the workings of conditioned reflex. We have programmed ourselves to respond in a certain way, and this response eventually becomes automatic, or at least largely beyond our conscious control. It is the jack-in-the-box effect that Bergson described so eloquently, a mechanization of our powers of free expression. Clowns have always demonstrated their tyrannical, almost hypnotic control of their audiences by beginning a characteristic gesture, then refusing to complete it, despite the frenzied urging of the audience. Their comic mastery is shown by their ability to tease and to titillate. The anticipation of the audience, either satisfied or frustrated but very much in evidence, becomes a motor activity, and one can observe the literal effects of empathy, as the audience unconsciously imitates or completes a gesture.

In the improvised scenarios of the Italian *commedia dell' arte* troupes of the Renaissance, the highly trained actors used traditional *lazzi* (or stage business) to define their set roles. The actors became famous (or notorious) for their *lazzi*, and these conventional gestures and bits of improvised action may have been inherited from the earliest Roman comedy. The clown's short baton (or slapstick) and bladder filled with dried peas, which were used in carefully prescribed ways to punctuate beatings, may have originated in some primitive Italic festival, where the scapegoat had to be soundly beaten before he was driven out. The blows are noisily administered, but they don't really hurt, and the clown, as expected, is not much perturbed by his ritual beating. More generally, but with a distinct symbolic relation, the slapstick or bladder may be used to indicate foolishness in the dialogue or action of others. It is the clown's protest against stupidity in persons of higher social standing, whom the clown cannot possibly touch. Beatings, or their aural equivalent, are entirely reversible in the comic action, which maintains its own sense of moral appropriateness and its own careful system of rewards and punishments. For the beater to be beaten is perfect poetic justice.

Literal repetition may involve certain tag lines or catch phrases that keep cropping up regardless of the context. The line has a life of its own apart from the character. The character, in fact, is defined as the user of a certain expression, just as one might say, "I recognize the phrase, but I don't remember the face," or, in Milton Berle's line, "You heckled me twenty years ago. I never forget a suit." The mad Trouble-all in Jonson's *Bartholomew Fair* threads his way through the play always asking, with unchanging persistence, "Have you Justice Overdo's warrant?" He has been rendered lunatic by the law, and his question startles one and all without exception, even an innocent bystander making water against a wall. He is a Jonsonian "humors" character, with a single preoccupation endlessly repeated. One of the therapeutic aims of Jonson's comedy is to put characters out of their humor, to free them from the short-circuiting mechanism of repetition by which they are trapped, and to allow them to live spontaneously (and therefore humanly) again. Shakespeare's Corporal Nym in *Henry V* is making fun of Jonson when he constantly asserts, "That's the humor of it." Repetition is closely allied either with outright madness or with an intense and narrow persistence that renders a character something less than human and also makes a mockery of his free will.

Comedy often turns on a question of identity, and mistaken identity is therefore a favorite comic device. Identity can be more easily mistaken if it was never too strongly asserted, and the persons of comedy, unlike those in tragedy, are frequently interchangeable types. Their integral humanity has been exchanged for a self-operating mechanism, by which they become parts of a larger mechanized unit called the play, which is a microcosm of society. The comic action often moves toward an escape from standardization and the interchangeability of parts, but, as Bergson has so convincingly shown, the mechanization and the denial of free humanity generate the comic action. This makes most comic plots highly schematic.

Consider the grievous natural dilemma of twins. By definition, they are a living problem in mistaken identity, and they express organically the mechanism of repetition. As Orsino says at the end of *Twelfth Night*, when he finally sees the twins, Sebastian and Viola, together: "One face, one voice, one habit [costume], and two persons— / A natural perspective that is and is not" (5.1.216–17). Suddenly, all the plot complications are resolved by a device that might seem hopelessly unpersuasive. Plautus delighted in using twins for farcical effect, especially in *The Menaechmus Twins*, which is one of the sources for Shakespeare's *Comedy of Errors*, but Shakespeare goes Plautus one (or two) better by doubling the twins into a pair of twin masters waited on by a pair of twin servants. In Plautus's *Amphitryon* there is a special ironic effect from the artificial twins played by the gods, Jove and Mercury, imitating mortals, Amphitryon and Sosia. Mortal and immortal are twinned, which creates a histrionic rather than a natural repetition, since the gods always remain distinct from the mortals they impersonate. The ironic perspective is beautifully exploited by Giraudoux in *Amphitryon 38* (or the thirty-eighth version of the Amphitryon theme).

In Shakespeare's *Comedy of Errors*, the simultaneous presence of two pairs of twins stepping in and out of each others' lives encourages a feeling of hysteria and frenzy that grows more hectic at each encounter. At a certain point in the action, Antipholus of Syracuse must either escape back to his ship, as his servant advises, or accept the practical consequences of what seems to be a permanently mistaken identity. Since he is always unaccountably on the receiving end—bags of money are thrust into his hands, a gold chain is pressed upon him, a lovely woman insists that she is his wife and importunes him to dinner and to bed—it is not difficult for Antipholus of Syracuse to make his decision. He cheerfully accepts the world of dreams, of fantasy, and of magic as his provisional reality, and he relinquishes, at least for the time being, any claim to the less generous reality that he knows to be true. Mere truth cannot withstand the shower of gold, and the speech of Antipholus is a manifesto of the comic hero:

> *To me she speaks, she moves me for her theme;*
> *What, was I married to her in my dream?*
> *Or sleep I now, and think I hear all this?*
> *What error drives our eyes and ears amiss?*
> *Until I know this sure uncertainty,*
> *I'll entertain the offered fallacy. (2.2.182–87)*

By his willingness to believe in a beneficent falsehood ("fallacy"), Antipholus of Syracuse takes what is "offered" in good spirit and without complaining about the violation of some literal but narrow truth.

Antipholus of Ephesus is not so fortunate. Everything is constantly being taken away from him, so that it comes as no surprise when he refuses to accept a reality that has suddenly and capriciously turned against him. We cannot demand stoic acceptance from the victims of mistaken identity. Servants and masters often exchange roles, as in Farquhar's *Beaux' Stratagem*, Shakespeare's *Taming of the Shrew*, Goldsmith's *She Stoops to Conquer*, and many other comedies, and the humor arises from an ironic repetition of attitudes and remarks from one role to another. The servant is masterfully the master and the master is masterfully the servant. There is a natural appropriateness in the reversal of roles that defies the rights of birth and social position.

Comedy flourishes on repetition. It seems to offer us a fixed and secure point in an otherwise mad and dislocated world. By the omniscient pleasures of dramatic irony, we know who the twins are, and we are always aware of the distinction between master and servant, god and mortal. Perhaps some clever director will take away our comfortable dramatic irony and force us to see a single actor playing both twins (if that is possible), or prevent us from distinguishing between the twins by some notable difference in costume (feather or no feather, different-colored hats). As a final possibility, he might introduce a distinction that is completely inconsistent; that is, both twins wear the feather at different times in order to confuse us. Real twins apparently delight in existential games like these on the fringes of the question of identity, where the comic implications shade over into the metaphysical theme of the double. When a twin chooses to make love to the "wrong" person, we are thrust into a situation that is not only farcical, but also absurd, grotesque, surreal, and perhaps cruel, in the special sense in which Peter Brook practices comedy of cruelty, as in his devastating production of Weiss's *Marat-Sade*. It is a jape, but also disturbing; by being disturbed, we tend to laugh excessively and without adequate provocation.

As noted earlier, repetition seems to have predictable, neurological effects. We anticipate repetition and prepare ourselves for the impact; when it occurs, we experience the shock of recognition. But the repetition is never the same as the preceding or initial episode. It seems to grow, to burgeon, to proliferate, as the enlarging foot in Ionesco's *Amédée* may stand in as a baleful metaphor for the art of comedy, or the moving men's delivery of furniture in the *New Tenant*, that fills, overfills, and ultimately chokes off all possibility of continuing life. Ionesco is a master of the overwhelming climax, of the climax that outdoes all other climaxes by the sheer prolongation and supererogation of repetition. The effect is not merely one of accumulation, but of snowballing, with an acceleration that sweeps us along to a triumphant (or catastrophic) conclusion. When this kind of comedy succeeds, the feeling of acceleration it produces is completely physical and could be measured by changes in pulse, respiration, skin temperature, etc. The physiological effect is comparable to that of suspense in melodrama, because we are eager to speed up an already speeded-up action and push it to its inevitable end. Joe Orton's *What the Butler Saw* moves inexorably to the apocalyptic exit of all the characters up the ladder, "*weary, bleeding, drugged, and drunk . . . into the blazing light,*" which may be the ultimate joke topping all the lesser jokes leading up to it.

The method is that of successful farce, of which the French playwright Georges Feydeau (1862–1921) is the undisputed master. The original complications are endlessly complicated, and the initial situation seems to engage in comic mitosis like an amoeba. Lovers are paired, tripled, quadrupled, but in disguises and with obstructions that render them impenetrable to each other. Persons are stowed away in closets, trunks, Murphy beds, drapes, pianos, etc., so that the stage scene at any particular moment is bursting with hiding places. Alarms suddenly go off to indicate the fumbling consummation of infidelities, but the parties are wrong, and a top hat and trousers are mysteriously thrown from an obscure hotel bedroom. Lights go on and off, as if they had a will of their own, and a prosthetic palette is constantly appearing and disappearing with remarkable effect on the speech of its wearer. Not only are letters delivered to the wrong persons, but they are also written by the wrong persons in a seeming fit of absent-mindedness or amnesia. The police are sometimes the villains, and the villains are usually exceptionally soft-hearted and sentimental and given to copious tears. Characters are reduced suddenly to impotence or inflamed to raging satyriasis by certain phrases and expressions of a strikingly literary flavor.

Reality (or its reverse) is entirely unpredictable in Feydeau, or perhaps it is utterly predictable, since the pattern of repetition and of development is so artfully calculated. It is a game that always ends in a wildly accelerated climax. When it is successful, as it usually is, the audience is completely taken in by the illusion. It participates in the joyous abandon of acceleration, and it may undergo that ecstatic experience the French call *fou rire*—mad, uncontrollable, orgiastic laughter, which is laughter in its most involuntary (and therefore purest) form.

Comedies are expected to end happily, with feasting, dancing, drinking, revelry, and the promise of offspring.

Just as tragedies end in death, so comedies typically end in marriage. Thus the structure of comedy satisfies (or seems to satisfy) two contrary impulses at once: (1) the anarchic and insistent urge for pleasure, in which love and sex, beautiful girls, food and drink, a warm bath and an oily massage all play an essential role, and (2) the integration of the comic hero into the society he has rebelled against. His lusts are institutionalized in marriage, and the war between youth and age, sons and fathers, which begins so many comedies in the tradition of Plautus, now ceases. By marrying, the comic hero becomes an official member of the very society he set out to destroy, and the scurrilous boasts of sexual prowess on the marriage night and the ability to engender half a dozen strong-backed boys are only a final echo of horny self-indulgence, now merged into the complacency of the solid citizen. The promise of offspring assures the stability and continuance of the society. The father-to-be has sown his wild oats and is now ready to assume adult responsibilities.

But at the end of comedy all these admirable social vows and promises have not yet been put into practice, and the feasting and revelry that take place are more to celebrate the natural culmination of youth than the more sober phase that is to follow. So the end of comedy is also a ritual ending, which makes it a beautiful and nostalgic moment that more than justifies any grossness or any excess. It is a moment of license as well as freedom. Thus, after the dénouement in Plautus's *Pseudolus* there is a remarkable episode in which the clever slave who engineered the plot struts about drunkenly and lords it over his humble and admiring master, who has, in fact, been the butt of the comedy. For the moment, Pseudolus is the Lord of Misrule, but the revelry cannot be prolonged. Tomorrow Pseudolus will be a slave again and the rules and assumptions of everyday reality will once more apply. The climactic moment of comedy is an exception, a holiday mood in which the rules are suspended and anything goes. The point is that the participants in the comic ending recognize its exceptional, ritualistic character and act according to the special dictates of the festive impulse. They are consciously sentimental and self-indulgent.

We are speaking, of course, about the values of a male society, in which the girls, no matter how beautiful, do not play a decisive role. No matter how witty, they are programmed into motherhood without any elaborate prior consultation. Congreve's brilliant heroine, Millamant, in *The Way of the World* (1700), insists on legal stipulations to guarantee her personal freedom when she is married: "Come to dinner when I please; dine in my dressing room when I'm out of humor, without giving a reason. To have my closet [private room] inviolate; to be sole empress of my tea table, which you must never presume to approach without first asking leave. And lastly, wherever I am, you shall knock at the door before you come in" (IV, 197–201). Mirabell has his own counter-conditions, but everything turns on the understanding that childbearing is the natural and indisputable function of a wife. The studied ease and artifice of Mirabell and Millamant on this subject show the strength of their assumptions:

> MIRABELL. *Item*, when you shall be breeding—
> MILLAMANT. Ah! name it not.
> MIRABELL. Which may be presumed, with a blessing on our endeavors—
> MILLAMANT. Odious endeavors! (IV, 230–34)

Millamant agrees with what she cannot oppose, and her wit is merely a way of accommodating herself to her social obligations.

There is no way for the structure of comedy to avoid the prevailing mores, and the end of comedy, which is a much more conservative genre than tragedy, must reflect the ends of society. No pun is intended on "end" and "ending," although it is obvious that the endings of comedy enforce orthodoxy. Plautus often makes the lady and the pot of gold scarcely distinguishable as prizes—chattel prizes—offered the male lead as a reward for his enterprising masculinity. As a matter of fact, the young man in Plautus is usually just as obscure as the young girl, and once he has convincingly explained his needs to the comic slave or parasite, his active role is effectively over. The girl is presented to him at the end, like a beribboned gift package, almost without any effort on his part.

We all know the social rules that relegate women to a passive role, yet comedy, as George Meredith so clearly understood in his *Essay on Comedy* (1877), is in many ways a celebration of the power and the wit of women. This is rarely announced openly, yet women in comedy engage in guerrilla warfare with the official values and mores. Shakespeare's *Taming of the Shrew* is usually played with an ironic ending. Does Petruchio really tame Katherine into a submissive, obedient wife, or does the wily Kate merely pretend to be a model wife in order to preserve her own mastery? Has Petruchio unwittingly taught her more than he intended and revealed the true secret of social life? These ambiguous possibilities are left open at the end of the play, which hardly seems the pious domestic tract that it pretends to be. Shakespeare seems to approach some of the subtleties of the true question of "mastrye" ("mastery"), or who wears the pants, which Chaucer so cunningly and brilliantly argued in the stories of the "Marriage Group" in *The Canterbury Tales*. The male triumph expected by society is often only a hollow victory, a mere appearance, while the woman exercises power from behind the public scene.

On the question of women in comedy, we have to face the fact that social ends and comic endings may not coincide. Comedy is not, after all, social propaganda, and the women are consistently wittier and more intelligent than the men, especially in the domain of love and sex. The girls in comedy are never rendered speechless fools or babbling idiots by love, as the men often are. Love seems to hit the men like a stunning blow on the head, whereas the girls are usually made keener, more acute, more charming, and more independent by the powers of affection. Look at Aristophanes' *Lysistrata*, which is more than 2400 years old, but still displays an uncanny understanding of women and their ability to resist oppressive institutions. The men are dolts in that play, entirely crippled by a literal and figurative swelling.

According to the comedy of humors, associated with Ben Jonson, the purpose of comedy is to purge socially unacceptable behavior. The "humorous" character is put out of his humor. In other words, his madness is cured, he is no longer preoccupied with the fixed idea with which he began, and he is willing to give up certain offensive idiosyncrasies of behavior and rejoin polite society. But the theory is constantly subverted in practice, and the humorous character ranges far beyond the social tics and mannerisms that offend his peers.

The theory could only be perfectly illustrated by a comic dramatist who was an apologist for the tedious values of social equilibrium, but Jonson, Chapman, and even the comic dramatists of the Restoration refuse to honor mere propriety in the face of vigorous originality, and their witty characters are constantly making fun of the very mores by which they act. It is ultimately a matter of the right style rather than the right values. Social critics are generally blind to the fact that even the most rigid comedy of humors and comedy of manners are satirical rather than propagandistic, and the prevailing manners of the wits are by no means intended as a social model. The butts, like Jonson's Amorous La Foole (in *Epicoene*) and Etherege's Sir Fopling Flutter (in *The Man of Mode*) are notable eccentrics and originals, who exercise a powerful attraction on their detractors, and who are, after all, the cause that wit is in other men.

A normative, moralistic theory of comedy is bound to have difficulties with endings, where the restoration of the social equilibrium is very imperfectly and very partially carried out. The endings pay lip service to conventional pieties, but that is something different from the strenuous realities of the comic action. Comedy is expected to have a happy ending, and it generally produces one with a minimum of effort and probability. In tragedy, the ending is crucial, and the whole action moves inexorably to the death or deaths that must conclude it. The tragic ending is climactic and of high significance, but in comedy it is difficult to produce a convincing resolution. Since comedy is so highly plot-oriented—so highly artful or artificial, as we might say—there is no chance of devising an ending that will seem natural and fitting. In fact, the ending is likely to be the most artificial element in the entire action, as coincidences are introduced, chance meetings are rigged, and the old strawberry mark (and other "tokens of recognition," as Aristotle calls them in the *Poetics*) are flashed before the wearied eyes of an unbelieving audience.

The normal reaction is to laugh at these wild improbabilities and accept them only as triumphs of witty ingenuity—the more far-fetched the better. We know we are being mercilessly fooled, but we would like to admire the playwright's cunning and audacity and let him wrap up his action any way he chooses. But the conclusion of the comic action violates the feeling we have that comedy is dimensionless, nontemporal, infinitely extensible, and not amenable to finite solutions or resolutions. We accept the ending as a literary convention without in any way longing for it or even desiring it, because we don't want the comic action to terminate. This is quite different from the expectations that govern jokes, where the punch line defines the experience and is, literally, what everyone has been waiting for.

Comedies end with the creation of what Northrop Frye calls a "new society," or at least a restoration of harmony, common sense, and civilized behavior, but certain characters are rigidly excluded from this new order. The villains of comedy, who keep the plot moving, must finally either be totally converted by well-placed holy men or private miracles (as in *As You Like It*), or else be summarily dismissed. Soreheads, bad losers, spoilsports, wet blankets, wallflowers, and other enemies of good fun and mutual jollification are to be classed with comic villains, as is anyone who refuses to be put out of his humor or to lend a helping hand in the common merriment. The refusal of a drink proffered with appropriate ceremony is enough to forfeit eternally the rewards of the happy ending. The casting out of misfits at the end is the way that comedy asserts the exclusiveness of its world and all its special prerogatives. In the showdown, there are no middle categories and special cases: the characters are either in or out of the comic resolution.

Shakespeare makes a special point of getting rid of stiff characters who cannot properly be assimilated into the happy ending. Surely Malvolio in *Twelfth Night* is one of those harsh egotists who can never be mollified, and his threat of revenge on the comic manipulators is meant as a hollow boast, which is certainly not intended to draw a tear from his conscience-stricken tormentors or from a tender and sensitive audience. They are all glad to be rid of him. Jaques, too, in *As You Like It*, is a rather nasty type, full of ridiculously sentimental effusions and a studied melancholy. No one will miss him in the new regime; his thoughtfulness is sickly and perverse. Shylock is a more difficult case, but he is so harshly punished and so resentful at the end that he must be forcibly expelled from the romantic world of new lovers and recently consummated marriages. He is simply out of place in the comic ending, and to suggest that he dies of a broken heart, as did the British TV production with Laurence Olivier, is a vulgar attack on the delightfully arbitrary happy ending. The new society of Belmont and Venice, floating on Pythagorean theories of celestial music, is all the more glamorous for the exclusion of Shylock.

To make others laugh is to assert one's power over them, and to laugh oneself is to express an ultimate freedom, so that the audience has it both ways, by identifying with the comic hero, and by choosing to laugh at his merry pranks and witty sayings. Comic catharsis produces the happy ending, which is both fortunate and joyous, and we identify with the newly reconciled and harmonious society of the dénouement. Out of complication comes pleasure, and we rejoice in difficulties overcome. As some directors have discovered, the audience at a comedy should be encouraged to participate directly in the festive ending. They don't want the hard-won illusion to be broken or the mood to be spoiled. Dancing, drinking, and revelry are in order. Peter Brook's production of *A Midsummer Night's Dream* at Stratford-on-Avon finished with a great mass of balloons being released into the audience, as the actors walked down the aisles and shook hands with the pleased and flattered spectators. It was a beautiful moment, and many in the audience were inspired to continue the mood of comic celebration outside the theater and long into the night.

IV

Forms of Comedy: Farce, Tragic Farce, Burlesque, Comedy of Manners, Satire, and Festive Comedy

Since comedy is such a highly formal and conventional art, comic writers think in terms of a few basic genres and types of comedy, especially those with a long and well developed tradition. The tendency is to limit the possibilities, to prefer variations on well known types to the innovation of new forms and new approaches. The comic audience needs to feel comfortable before it can respond freely and enthusiastically, so that any account of the categories of stage comedy depends on the values of the audience. Those who laugh establish norms for what is praiseworthy and what is ridiculous, and the comic playwright understands how to tease and flatter his audience.

If moral reformation is the real purpose of comedy, as classical and neoclassical critics have so strenuously insisted, the changes that may be wrought in the audience are compressed within a surprisingly narrow range. Common sense informs us that the message of comedy is usually "Be Happy" rather than "Be Good," although moral good and good will may be generated as a by-product of good spirits. The expression of comic morality is usually limited to the end of the play, where conventional expectations are fulfilled and the world is a better place to live in than it was at the beginning of the play—or at least a clearer, more lucid, more rational, and more purposive place. The true subject of comedy is manners rather than morals, and we are more concerned with how people live than why, whereas in tragedy we are almost immediately engaged in questions of good and evil. That is why comedy, as it is usually practiced, serves rather to enforce the prevailing mores than to establish any new society based on true virtue and the claims of the ideal.

The six forms of comedy we will discuss all have certain characteristics in common. They all ridicule absurdities that isolate their practitioners from the norms of social life. They all are preoccupied with language as an expressive medium, and they all use parody or travesty as a ready means of social criticism. They all are self-conscious about acting; the comic hero is always someone acutely aware of playing a role. They all postulate the triumph of wit over the vicissitudes of everyday, material life. These six types of comedy are by no means an exclusive group; they are all interrelated and freely overlap each other's territory. Tragicomedy will not be considered here as a separate, historical form, because it is so deeply mingled with the techniques and values of tragedy, but the section on tragic farce includes some account of tragicomic materials.

*A farce is a comedy with an extravagant
plot in which anything can happen. The
characters are developed by quirks and
eccentricities rather than according to any
believable, psychological truth.*

Farce is one of the central topics of this book, and points already
made about the mechanisms of comedy, often illustrated by examples from farce, will not be repeated. Farce may be the purest,
quintessential comedy, since it so rigorously excludes any sentiment at all, especially feelings of sympathy, compassion, or empathy for the characters. It is also unintellectual, unpsychological,
and uncomplex, with energetic, dream-like characters pursuing
their impulses and gratifications with an amazing singleness of purpose. Farce is the only kind of comedy in which there is frenzied
simplicity, which may be why all other kinds of comedy bear a
type resemblance to farce. The prevailing mood is one of a world
gone mad, or at least a world where wish-fulfillment fantasies are
acted out by the characters. In farce anything is possible, and the
audience expects surprises, transformations, quick changes of heart
(and costume), trapdoors suddenly opening, revelations in closets,
remarkable concealments and discoveries, and a general feeling of
wildness and hysteria building to a grand, accelerated climax.

We laugh when the servant-clown is beaten by his master, and
beatings are as natural an expression of emotion in farce as tears
might be in sentimental comedy or melodrama. The beating is a
conventional expedient of those in authority. When the Dromio
twins in *The Comedy of Errors* insist on mixing themselves up with
irrational stubbornness, their masters, the Antipholus twins, only
know how to confront the larger question of identity by resorting
to beatings of a wholly spontaneous and unforced—even good-
hearted, if not actually hearty—nature. When in doubt use blows,
as if the blows were a way of striking back at a recalcitrant and
confusing reality and forcing it to conform with common sense.
Blows are a normal response in farce to the ubiquitous presence of
unreason.

Another way to define farce is to call it a play in the style of
Plautus, the great Roman comic writer who lived from about 254
to 184 B.C. Twenty of Plautus's plays survive, all adapted from
Greek originals, and he developed the formulas of New Comedy
with an unerring genius for what would appeal to a popular audience. His plots are always farfetched but extremely simple to follow: the plotter, usually a servant or parasite (general factotum or
"freeloader," as Lionel Casson translates it), is able to manipulate
the action with persistence, resourcefulness, and cunning so that
the old father, the pimp, and all rich, important, and pompous
men, are tricked and swindled by the young lovers. Everything is
done in the spirit of fun, and all malice is neutralized by the happy
ending. In *Pseudolus* the cruel, grasping, and intensely materialistic
pimp, Ballio, is discomforted and forced to give up the girl Calidorus adores, and Simo, the father of Calidorus, is also made to
look foolish—all by the clever machinations of Pseudolus, Simo's
slave, who knows how to seize the occasion and improvise a brilliant victory out of almost certain defeat. Pseudolus is endowed
with the grotesque physical distortion associated with clowns: *"an
enormous head . . . along with a bulging belly and a pair of oversize feet."*
There is an old comic tradition that the clown should be physically
set apart from other men, that he should look "clownish."

In *The Menaechmus Twins*, everything turns on the farcical assumption that no matter how overwhelming the evidence, the
twins will never recognize that they are confronting each other.
Menaechmus of Syracuse is actually searching the world for his
lost twin brother, so that it is especially difficult to understand how
he can ignore all the signs that present themselves to him in Epi-
damnus. But this built-in innocence or thickness of perception or
comic blindness and obliquity—stupidity, to give it its right
name—is an important characteristic of farce. The characters are
all wound up or set to act in a certain way, and they are remarkably resistant to reality, insensitive to the obvious truth that sur-
rounds them, inflexible, and unadaptable—perfect models, in
other words, for Bergson's theory of comedy as a mechanical in-
trusion into the free-flowing, vital forces of life. This stiffness is
what gives farcical characters their charm. They are true to themselves and not easily influenced by any transient truths they may
happen to encounter in the course of the action.

Even when the Menaechmus twins finally meet toward the end of the play, they don't immediately fall into each other's arms (as we would expect in romantic comedy) and thank the good fortune that has reunited them. That's not the way farce works. We still have a good bit of legalistic dialogue in which the twins produce their tokens of recognition, including the names of their mother and father, and the fact that Menaechmus of Syracuse used to be called Sosicles. Nothing is taken for granted, and there is a powerful assumption in all of farce that mere physical appearance is the most deceptive illusion of all. Othello's compulsion to have "ocular proof" would be very much at home in farce, and Iago has many of the qualities of the wily servant, who knows how to insinuate himself into a winning argument.

Shakespeare's *Comedy of Errors* doubles the twins, masters and servants, Antipholuses and Dromios, without necessarily doubling the fun. Shakespeare was not fully comfortable in farce, and this is his only attempt in the Plautine genre. Plautus is bold and direct and uncompromising, whereas Shakespeare feels the need to offer explanations. Magic, witchcraft, the world of dreams and enchantment enter significantly into *The Comedy of Errors*, as if to make its preposterous assumptions more credible. But Plautus doesn't trouble himself with questions of credibility. His characters are perfectly normal persons from ordinary, middle-class Roman households. There is nothing strange or romantic about them at all, except that they just happen to be involved in wild schemes and incredible disguises, and we see them on stage busily acting out their fantasies.

Shakespeare's *Comedy of Errors* is not quite a farce because it is so thoroughly suffused with romantic-poetic ideas. Thus, Antipholus of Syracuse conceives his quest for his long-lost twin in the beautiful image of the anonymous drop of water:

> *I to the world am like a drop of water*
> *That in the ocean seeks another drop,*
> *Who, falling there to find his fellow forth,*
> *Unseen, inquisitive, confounds himself.* (1.2.35–38)

This is foreign to the spirit of Plautus, whose characters have the very limited, practical vision of persons committed to daily life. In the "drop of water" image, Shakespeare explores the question of identity on which *The Comedy of Errors* turns; in *The Menaechmus Twins* Plautus never lets such puzzling, metaphysical questions arise.

Machiavelli's *Mandragola* (about 1518) is much more energetically in the spirit of Plautus. Young Callimaco must have Lucrezia, the beautiful young wife of Messer Nicia, the aging lawyer—he must make love with her or perish. It is all that simple (or simplified). His motives are never explored, nor are they amenable to any kind of analysis. It is purely a matter of sexual passion without the slightest concession to morality, religion (Fra Timoteo, in fact, panders to him), money, or any other complicating factor. This gives the play a feeling of cynical good will, since Callimaco means well and doesn't intend to harm anyone or hurt anyone's feelings. He even makes ingenious use of the husband to bring him to the wife, and the husband virtually joins the two together in bed. Callimaco is a good-natured fellow without any desire to lord it over anyone or to take unfair advantage. He merely wants to sat- isfy an obsessive passion that he doesn't pretend to understand; once the plot gets underway, the action moves swiftly and inexora- bly to its preordained conclusion. It's no wonder that Machiavelli's farce has been compared to his manual of italianate statecraft, *The Prince*, since both are preoccupied with the techniques of moving means to ends. Perhaps there is something inherently farcical, as Bergson insisted in his essay on laughter, in the mechanization of life and the life processes to the achievement of narrowly defined goals. Being outside the control of reason (at least in plays), sex can function as an autonomous system pressing valiantly to farcical gratification.

In the plays of Georges Feydeau (1862–1921), who is certainly the greatest modern writer of farces, sex becomes the main mo- tivating device, as characters pursue each other in and out of draw- ing rooms, hotels of assignation, and revolving beds. There is a frenzy of activity in a Feydeau farce, all turning on sexual pursuit and its associated complications, such as marriage, jealousy, honor, love, and eloquent speeches. Lust is everywhere assumed, and the atmosphere is heavy with satyriasis and nymphomania (both usually feigned), but consummation and climax always elude the ardent pursuers. The frustrations and surprises of the sexual game are mollified by wit, and the characters are always ready with an apt rejoinder or a stunning bit of repartee. In Feydeau, being partially unclothed stimulates the comic imagination.

In *Keep an Eye on Amélie*, Amélie is a former coquette now turned cocotte, or "loose woman" as it is generally defined—but the promiscuity is selective and professional, and a cocotte is more a "kept woman" than a call girl. The very desirable heroine is pursued simultaneously and concomitantly by the following lovers or mock-lovers: Etienne, her official boy friend who lives with her; Marcel, who pretends to marry her (and actually does) in order to fulfill the terms of a will; and the Prince of Palestria, who makes love to her at various odd moments purely on the strength of his official dignities. Van Putzeboum, the godfather of Marcel, has an interest in Amélie that may or may not be avuncular, or that may be more avuncular at some points in the play than at others. The general atmosphere of the play is turbulent, with new and extraordinary surprises popping up at every moment. In the mock-marriage ceremony, for example, the mayor is supposed to be played by Toto Bejard, and much is made of the fact that the supposed Toto has feigned a large growth or protuberance on his forehead. This is considered the height of wit, but it turns out that the lump is real and the mayor is real, too, and Marcel and Amélie have really been married.

The genius of Feydeau lies in his enormous inventiveness. He shows an exuberance of imagination that can transform the tired formulas and stock situations of farce into something bursting with vitality. And Feydeau understood how to organize a complex action toward a brilliant climax. In *A Flea in Her Ear*, the assignations at the Hotel Coq d'Or in Montretout (The Golden Cock in Showall) are multiplied so effectively that the whole action vibrates with hysterical movement. Raymonde, the jealous wife of Victor Emmanuel Chandebise, is trying to trap her husband, while Romain Tournel, her husband's assistant, is pursuing her. Raymonde is willing to be Tournel's mistress, if only to satisfy the triangulations of the plot, "But not to go to bed with you! Do you think I'm a prostitute?"

Meanwhile, the rheumatic Baptistin, a relative of the hotel

owner, keeps popping in and out on a revolving bed activated by a button, and a madly lustful German, Herr Schwarz, avidly pursues with clipped orders in German, all females. Feydeau pointedly uses foreign accents and foreign languages as a vehicle for his most profound irrationality, as if the speakers, by abandoning French, had deliberately chosen to abandon reason. Camille Chandebise, the master's nephew, appears at the Coq d'Or with Antoinette, the wife of Etienne, the butler, and an additional complication arises when he loses his artificial palate and reverts to speaking in a stage harelip accent. Etienne, the husband-butler, then enters, followed by Madame Lucienne Homenides de Histangua, a friend of Raymonde's who obliged her by writing a letter of assignation to her husband, M. Chandebise. Señor Homenides, a frantically impetuous and insanely jealous Latin American, then follows, ready to kill his wife and her supposed lover. When M. Chandebise finally comes on the scene, he is immediately mistaken by everyone without exception for the alcoholic Poche, a servant in the hotel who formerly served under the command of the owner—an error which activates its own set of consequences. All of these inflamed characters are generously mixed together, with additional involvements with the hotel staff, so that the scene ends in an apocalyptic frenzy, which may be the effect that farce is most eager to produce. There is a literal fullness and overfullness to the bursting point, as in the stateroom scene in the Marx Brothers' *A Night at the Opera* (see Figure 8).

Joe Orton's exuberant farce, *What the Butler Saw* (1969), also ends with an apocalyptic climax, as the much-abused and partially clothed characters ascend through the skylight: *"They pick up their clothes and weary, bleeding, drugged and drunk, climb the rope ladder into the blazing light."* Orton is a brilliant epigrammatist in the style of Oscar Wilde, and the play is full of self-conscious gag lines. Mrs. Prentice's dialogue with the mad Dr. Rance is completely typical:

> MRS. PRENTICE. He [her husband, Dr. Prentice] had no sympathy for me when I complained of being assaulted by a page-boy at the Station Hotel.
> RANCE. What was the object of the assault?
> MRS. PRENTICE. The youth wanted to rape me.

Figure 8. Comic Fullness: The Marx Brothers in *A Night at the Opera* (Metro-Goldwyn-Mayer, 1935).

> *RANCE.* He didn't succeed?
> *MRS. PRENTICE.* No.
> *RANCE.* (*shaking his head*) The service in these hotels is dreadful.

As is the "dreadful" pun on "service."

What the Butler Saw is set in Dr. Prentice's private psychiatric clinic, which provides a farcical context for the play. It is never apparent whether any or all of the characters are either mad or sane, and the terms cease to have any identifiable meaning. In this setting, everything is possible. This is the proper mood of farce, and we are never meant to sympathize with the abused and exploited characters, including the innocent Geraldine, who is sent to Dr. Prentice by the Friendly Faces Employment Agency. At the very beginning of her job interview, she is asked to remove her clothes (which she never recovers) and to try out Dr. Prentice's new contraceptive device. After this brusque introduction, Geraldine continues to be victimized throughout the play. She is soon an involuntary patient in the psychiatric clinic and certified as insane. It is worth noting, among several farcical details that are never exploited, that Geraldine is carrying a small cardboard box which contains parts of "A recently erected statue of Sir Winston Churchill. . . . Parts of the great man were actually found embedded in my [Geraldine's] step-mother." Dr. Prentice's question, "Which parts?", is not answered until the very end of the play, and then only ambiguously.

Orton shamelessly parodies Victorian melodrama (as Wilde does in *The Importance of Being Earnest*). In contemporary farce, parody is an important vehicle for displacing any extraneous feelings of sympathy or sincerity. Everything must be seen, as it were, at several removes from the original, and the author is constantly poking fun at his own sophisticated awareness of what he is doing. The most skillful of modern parodists is undoubtedly Tom Stoppard, whose *Rosencrantz and Guildenstern Are Dead* is a brilliant pastiche of Shakespeare's *Hamlet*, as seen through the frightened eyes of Rosencrantz and Guildenstern, the two minor court flunkies marked out for death from the beginning. The parody is more sustained in *The Real Inspector Hound*, which intertwines characters and critics in a hopelessly banal Victorian murder mystery at Muldoon Manor, a "lovely old Queen Anne House," which, because of a "topographical quirk in the local strata," has "no roads leading from the Manor, though there *are* ways of getting *to* it, weather allowing." The dialogue is so consistently bright and witty that we are never sure which play we are actually in, especially when the theater reviewers, Moon and Birdboot, begin to have an active role in the main play. As the distinction between play and play-within-the-play disappears, and as the dialogue begins to be repeated by different characters, we see the inevitable and much wished-for murder of three drama critics enacted before our eyes.

But the play remains a farce because it so effectively isolates and insulates our feelings. The audience may feel quizzical about what is happening on stage, but it is kept at bay by the scintillating parody and not allowed to get involved. Stoppard has a wonderful ear for fake portentousness, as in Moon's intended review, which he shapes for us while the play is in progress and which he delivers in his special "public voice, a critic voice": "Let me at once say that it has *élan* while at the same time avoiding *éclat*. Having said that, and I think it must be said, I am bound to ask—does this play know where it is going?"

"*Élan*" and "*éclat*" mimic the fashionable words of bad academic criticism, and Moon continues to press for larger, pseudo-philosophical significances: "Does it, I repeat, declare its affiliations? There are moments, and I would not begrudge it this, when the play, if we can call it that, and I think on balance we can, aligns itself uncompromisingly on the side of life. *Je suis*, it seems to be saying, *ergo sum*. But is that enough? I think we are entitled to ask." The trite allusion to Descartes' "*Cogito ergo sum*" ("I think, therefore I am") reminds us of the more extended and more technical parody of contemporary metaphysics in Stoppard's *Jumpers*, where all the philosophers are also trained acrobats, or vice versa. Stoppard takes malicious pleasure in satirizing the knowing leers, asides, and rhetorical questions of learning, especially in its professional and academic aspect. His kind of farce is quite different from that of Plautus, especially in its verbal and literary sophistication, but the elaboration of the plot and the unbridled extravagance of the author's invention are similar in spirit. Stoppard and Orton are like Plautus in their commitment to wild, amoral, surprising, unmitigated, and frantic comedy.

In tragic farce, the themes and techniques of tragedy have been absorbed and comically transformed.

There is no firm or distinct line between farce and tragic farce, and dramatists like Joe Orton and Tom Stoppard can easily move from the older kind of exuberant, energetic farce into the newer type of metaphysical, grotesque, and tragicomic farce. Stoppard's *Rosen-crantz and Guildenstern Are Dead* quotes and parodies a much-accelerated and transformed *Hamlet*, to which the King's absurd and pathetic factotums serve both as audience and participants, and Joe Orton's *What the Butler Saw* blurs any distinction between sanity and madness, ending with an apocalyptic vision (or mock-vision). In tragic farce the audience is made to feel uneasy. It indulges in nervous and self-conscious laughter, because it is not sure how to interpret the play. Everything evokes contradictory impressions, so that the audience might eventually think that it is the victim of the playwright's practical joke—that it is being had or put on. The uncertainty of tone is cultivated by the author to produce a bewildering, if not also painful experience, as the play shifts unpredictably between the farcical and the tragic, and no way is offered to bridge the discontinuity.

Peter Handke's recent *Offending the Audience* carries this idea to a surrealistic extreme, although the notion of insulting and disorienting an audience by wit is familiar from nightclub and cabaret routines. Lenny Bruce was one of its great practitioners. By insult the empty, middle-class values of the audience are satirized and exploded. The theoretical aim is to purge the spectators, through their own laughter, of all their shoddy, narrow, materialistic notions. The comic catharsis is meant to be moral and political, but it usually goes beyond ethical norms to a feeling of weightless, euphoric wish fulfilment. Beyond the moral point of comedy lies the attractive dreamlike zone of pure impulse (and therefore of pure freedom).

T. S. Eliot was one of the first to define "tragic farce," although he doesn't use that particular phrase (which is, incidentally, the subtitle of Ionesco's play *The Chairs: une farce tragique*). In his short essay on Marlowe (1918), Eliot makes the point that the conventional, moral definition of tragedy derived from Aristotle's *Poetics* is irrelevant to *The Jew of Malta:*

> If one takes *The Jew of Malta* not as a tragedy, or as a
> "tragedy of blood," but as a farce, the concluding act
> becomes intelligible; and if we attend with a careful ear to
> the versification, we find that Marlowe develops a tone to

> suit this farce, and even perhaps that this tone is his most
> powerful and mature tone. I say farce, but with the
> enfeebled humour of our times the word is a misnomer; it
> is the farce of the old English humour, the terribly serious,
> even savage comic humour, the humour which spent its
> last breath in the decadent genius of Dickens.

"Terribly serious, even savage comic humour" would be a good
way to define "tragic farce," provided that we avoid the middle-class
paradox of "serious" comedy. Tragic farce is serious only in the
strength of its philosophical and existential commitment, not in any
directly moral sense.

This is a large claim for farce, but in a world in which the possibility of tragedy has ceased to exist—because belief in a rational
order has been lost—farce has taken over the territory usually
claimed for tragedy. It is thus the only dramatic form still viable in
an absurd universe. The metaphysical assumptions are well stated
by Friedrich Dürrenmatt in his essay, "Problems of the Theatre"
(1958). For Dürrenmatt, "Comedy alone is suitable for us. Our
world has led to the grotesque as well as to the atom bomb, and so
it is a world like that of Hieronymus Bosch whose apocalyptic
paintings are also grotesque. But the grotesque is only a way of
expressing in a tangible manner, of making us perceive physically
the paradoxical, the form of the unformed, the face of a world
without face. . . ." The real problem is how to find what used to
be called tragedy in the new, all-pervasive form of farcical comedy:
"But the tragic is still possible even if pure tragedy is not. We can
achieve the tragic out of comedy. We can bring it forth as a frightening moment, as an abyss that opens suddenly; indeed, many of
Shakespeare's tragedies are already really comedies out of which
the tragic arises." Comedy, then, may include tragedy, but not vice
versa, and it is only through comedy that we may still discover
some of the experience that used to be associated with tragedy.

Dürrenmatt's plays cultivate the broad, unexplained, extreme
situations of farce to create a sense of dislocation and disorientation
in ordinary reality. In *The Visit*, the immensely wealthy and all-
powerful Claire Zachanassian returns to her native Guellen and
offers the town one million dollars for the killing of Alfred Ill, her

youthful lover who deserted her many years ago. Claire is sur-
rounded by her trained retinue of Toby, Roby, Koby, and Loby
(whose names, we are told, are interchangeable), and husbands
VII, VIII, and IX, who, during the course of the play, keep being
substituted for each other, exchanging their caricatured roles. And
Claire herself is made almost entirely of synthetic parts and expensive prosthetic devices.

Once we see the townspeople in their new yellow, pointy shoes
(purchased on credit, of course), we know that the fate of Ill is
sealed, and Ill himself seems to consent to his inevitable martyr-
dom. The seemingly tragic situation appears ridiculous and banal,
as Hanna Arendt understood Eichmann's "banality of evil." What
happens is too mean and petty to qualify for tragedy, and free will
is merely a specter. The action can only be farcically tragic (or
tragically farcical), since all of the traditional seriousness of tragedy
has been removed. Claire is genial, nostalgic, and even sentimen-
tally romantic with Ill, who is incapable of any grand gesture (or
any gesture at all) to defy his fate, and all the townspeople are filled
with a *gemütlich* good will toward Ill and toward each other as they
prepare for the ritual slaughter.

The play is a fable of the Nazi era, but displaced, distanced, and
made manageable by its farcical form. Dürrenmatt seems to ask:
How else can one deal dramatically with events of such overwhelming horror? In *The Physicists*, the playwright probes the moral
responsibility of science by placing his physicists in a madhouse,
where they pretend to be mad, while the presiding psychiatrist,
Fräulein Doktor Mathilde von Zahnd, is actually a raving megalo-
maniac prepared to conquer the world. The physicists (including
two secret agents of foreign powers) are trapped by their own naive
assumption of the "normality" of their madhouse retreat.

Dürrenmatt is conscious of the larger significance of his comedy,
and especially of the way it appropriates themes that used to be associated with tragedy. The farcical handling allows for a playfulness—a malicious playfulness and self-indulgence—that disturbs
and confuses the audience and arouses, when successful, a feeling
of grotesque outrage. It is an outrage without any possibility of
relief, because old-fashioned notions of good and evil, reward and
punishment, have been severely upset and our moral sympathies

anesthetized. Thus, heroes and villains in the old sense disappear, and we have only well-meaning but ineffectual clowns, who are powerless either to understand or to change what is happening to them and around them. Free will is the most absurd illusion of all, and its exercise can only lead to the sort of errors, mistaken identities, and plot complications one finds in the farces of Plautus. There is, of course, a prevailing irony in Dürrenmatt, and he writes like a tragic playwright *manqué*, as if to warn us at every step: this is what has happened to tragedy in our time.

Samuel Beckett is similarly portentous. His plays are full of significant statements about "how it is," about endings, dissolution, decay, return to point zero, and the breakdown not only of all rational discourse, but also of the very possibility of existence on planet earth. Yet Beckett is also wonderfully witty and irreverent. His characters, *in extremis*, still make jokes, puns, epigrams, sing snatches of songs, and try to refine their style. Their metaphysical situation seems to inspire them with a new eloquence, or at least force them to use their wits when everything merely external has failed. When the comedian Bert Lahr—perhaps best known for his portrayal of the Cowardly Lion in *The Wizard of Oz* (see Figure 9)—acted Estragon in *Waiting for Godot*, he confessed that he had no idea at all what the character meant, but played it strictly for laughs in the old vaudeville style.

That was probably the secret of Bert Lahr's success, since *Waiting for Godot* is full of traditionally farcical routines based on hats, shoes, beatings, and other clownish conventions. The two tramps, Estragon and Vladimir, don't even have a bit of rope with which to hang themselves, but their existential despair is much relieved by their dialogue, in which they entertain each other with unexpected bits and pieces of knowledge and invention, as in the following:

> VLADIMIR. What do we do now?
> ESTRAGON. Wait.
> VLADIMIR. Yes, but while waiting.
> ESTRAGON. What about hanging ourselves?
> VLADIMIR. Hmmm. It'd give us an erection.
> ESTRAGON. (*highly excited*) An erection!

VLADIMIR. With all that follows. Where it falls mandrakes
grow. That's why they shriek when you pull them up.
Did you know that?
ESTRAGON. Let's hang ourselves immediately!
VLADIMIR. From a bough? (*They go towards the tree.*) I
wouldn't trust it.

Figure 9. Bert Lahr as the Cowardly Lion in *The Wizard of Oz*
(Metro-Goldwyn-Mayer, 1939); *The Museum of Modern Art / Film Stills Archive.*

This is the innate skepticism of the comic hero, for whom death has no guaranteed reality. Perhaps the characters are beyond death or in some limbo where death doesn't count and time has stopped. But the dialogue doesn't stop, and Estragon is suddenly remembering "the story of the Englishman in the brothel." In *Endgame*, Nagg the old father, tells, from his cozy ashcan, an elaborate version of the old joke about the tailor and the world, while Hamm, the son, is constantly correcting and editing his own discourse to make it more elegant: "Nicely put, that," he says to himself. Language, discourse, communication—these are the last activities left in a world that is rapidly ceasing to exist, and Beckett's characters are wonderfully self-conscious of their own witty futility. In the production of *Waiting for Godot* with Bert Lahr, the lines that provoked the most violent laughter were Vladimir's comment: "This is becoming really insignificant," with Estragon's answer: "Not enough." The audience laughed in relief at being able to share its anxious bewilderment with the characters on stage.

It is unfashionable to speak of Beckett as a writer of comedies, but he is our greatest practitioner of tragic farce; the comic expression of tragic themes comes naturally to him. Even in the somber *Happy Days*, where Winnie is buried "up to above her waist" in a mound of sand in Act I, then up to her neck in Act II, Ruth White made Winnie's monologue continuously funny. Like Dame Quickly in Shakespeare's Henry IV plays, Winnie has a gift for comic irrelevance, as she rummages in a large shopping bag and brings up the bits and pieces of her life. Despite her situation, Winnie is completely at home, completely domestic, without anxiety, and with a great zest for life. She brushes her teeth, puts on makeup, looks in her mirror, and goes through the routines of daily life as if nothing were amiss. With great effort she learns that her toothbrush is made of genuine pure hog's bristles, a discovery that gives her a moment of great happiness: "That is what I find so wonderful, that not a day goes by—(*smile*)—to speak in the old style—(*smile off*)—hardly a day, without some addition to one's knowledge however trifling, the addition I mean, provided one takes the pains."

Later, near the end of the play, Winnie is pleased with herself that she can remember words from an old, sentimental song: "That is what I find so wonderful, a part remains, of one's classics, to help one through the day." This is all splendidly appropriate, and Winnie's ease and perfect timing convince us that she is imbedded in the sand more for our entertainment than as any kind of existential punishment. She is relaxed and confidential, like the best clowns, and once the play begins she can say anything at all and hold our interest. Beckett makes much of the intense disparity between her immobile position and her vivid discourse. We are all the more ready to accept any Beckett situation, no matter how wild or far-fetched, because of our familiarity with farce. Krapp eating a banana in *Krapp's Last Tape*—he has, in fact, a secret passion for bananas, which he keeps locked in his desk—establishes a similar parallel with Eliot's Apeneck Sweeney (in "Sweeney Among the Nightingales"): "Apeneck Sweeney spreads his knees / Letting his arms hang down to laugh. . . ." But Krapp's bananas also offer an excellent opportunity for pantomime and comic stage business. As in all metaphor, the vehicle and the tenor cannot be separated.

To read tragic farce is almost as difficult as to read farce. Without the stage action, the dialogue often seems wooden and the characters lifeless, and the marvelous effects of acceleration and snowballing are hard to grasp from the words on the printed page. That is why the examples are drawn from Beckett as performed—where the text comes alive and the action and characters have their own consistency and unity of tone. The exclusively literary interpretation of Beckett tends to emphasize his symbolism and his "philosophy" at the expense of his comic genius.

This is equally true for Harold Pinter, who has become an instant classic in American university circles (and maybe to himself, too—his later work is full of heavy significances), while his histrionic skill and comic brilliance have been neglected. Pinter has a fine ear for ordinary speech, especially the most banal sort of colloquial speech. In Pinter's plays banality reaches its apotheosis, so that we need, for our own peace of mind, to postulate a menacing reality hidden behind the staggering emptiness of everyday discourse. The revue sketch *Last to Go* is a tiny masterpiece of almost pointless dialogue. An old newspaper seller is speaking to a barman in a coffee shop about which of his papers is the "last to go":

BARMAN. Sold your last then, did you?
MAN. Yes, my last 'Evening News' it was. Went about twenty to ten. *Pause.*
BARMAN. 'Evening News', was it?
MAN. Yes. *Pause.* Sometimes it's the 'Star' is the last to go.
BARMAN. Ah.
MAN. Or the . . . whatsisname.
BARMAN. 'Standard'.
MAN. Yes. *Pause.* All I had left tonight was the 'Evening News'. *Pause.*
BARMAN. Then that went, did it?
MAN. Yes. *Pause.* Like a shot. *Pause.*
BARMAN. You didn't have any left, eh?
MAN. No. Not after I sold that one.

We also learn that the old newspaper seller has been to Victoria to look for George, whom he couldn't locate, who may (or may not) have suffered very bad from arthritis, and who may (or may not) have left the area. That is the full intellectual sweep of *Last to Go*, yet the play makes a teasing and probably meaningless counterpoint between the last newspaper to go and the mysterious disappearance of George. Its range is so intensely narrow as to be virtually incomprehensible, except in its free-floating implications. The sketch is more a model for dialogue or a conversation manual in the tradition of Swift's *A Compleat Collection of Genteel and Ingenious Conversation*. The tediousness, repetitiveness, explicitness, false logic, didacticism, and unbearable cuteness somehow manage to be appealing and unforgettable.

Pinter usually works in the broader and more traditional style of farce, as in his creation of the gangster Goldberg in *The Birthday Party*, who is constantly evoking the warm verities of Jewish family life. The ruthless Goldberg is drenched in unexpected sentimentality (what we would call "schmaltz"): "Up the street, into my gate, inside the door, home. 'Simey!' my old mum used to shout, 'quick before it gets cold.' And there on the table what would I see? The nicest piece of gefilte fish you could wish to find on a plate." Later it is "The nicest piece of rollmop and pickled cucumber you could wish to find on a plate." Goldberg is not a hypocrite, but merely an exuberant speaker, and he wishes his audience to share his expansive enthusiasm. He looks upon himself as a successful businessman, very persuasive and very devoted to the values of duty, home, and personal loyalty.

Pinter often makes his plays turn on farcical transformations, as in *A Slight Ache*, where the husband and the contemptible matchseller literally change roles at the end, according to the whim of the sexually unsatisfied wife. In *The Lover*, the proper married couple we see at the beginning suddenly become the frenzied, bongo-playing, sex-crazed lovers, who meet furtively in their own home for several inflamed afternoons a week. No explanations are offered, and we accept the situation as an imaginative comic device, with the proviso that we accept it only if it works. Pinter energizes the device by broad contrasts between the two worlds, each with its own special costume and speech. In *The Dumb Waiter*, two professional killers on an assignment suddenly begin to receive menu orders from a dumb waiter they discover in their basement room. They don't question the mysterious reality they have been taught to obey, and they hasten to send up makeshift substitutes for "Macaroni Pastitsio" and "Ormitha Macarounada." The play ends with one of the killers about to kill the other, which is presumably the assignment he has just received through the speaking tube next to the dumb waiter.

The play is frightening in its impact but not in its dialogue, which ranges over a wide variety of impossibly banal subjects, including bits from the newspaper that are read out, and a heated grammatical discussion over the correctness of the figure of speech, "to light the kettle," when we mean "to light the gas." Pinter teases his audience with fragments from daily life, but so removed from any meaningful context that they have an intense, surrealistic vividness. The humor arises from a farcical shock of recognition, by which we become aware of a terrifying absurdity in our ordinary existence. Is it poetic or is it banal? It's like those sculptured boxes of Joseph Cornell or Kurt Schwitters' "Merzbilder" collages—we discover a new reality in the most familiar objects when they are juxtaposed in a work of art, but the "new reality" is an illusion produced by a new context. The objects are all, by definition, out of context, so that the new reality must necessarily be distorted and radically different from its original configuration.

Burlesque comedy mocks the moral and stylistic pretensions of tragedy and romance.

Burlesque is a form of sustained parody, designed especially to ridicule the tragic high style. It is the most self-conscious kind of comedy, and it often uses a play within the play—the object of the burlesque—for which the frame play provides a satirical commentary. The main play thus functions as a vehicle for literary criticism—not just literary criticism in the narrow, technical sense, but a demonstration of good manners and good taste. The sentimentality of exaggerated feelings is an offense against literary standards. False pathos is rendered as bathos, which is one of the chief resources of burlesque: the sentiments are inappropriate and incongruous for the characters, as in Gay's *The Beggar's Opera* (1728), where thieves and whores ape the polished banalities and moral platitudes of upper-class society. In burlesque there is always a clearly defined perspective from which to focus the parody. Although Stoppard doesn't write formal and sustained burlesque, he delights in confusing the perspective between play, audience, and play-within-the-play, so that Rosencrantz and Guildenstern are both players and audience in *Rosencrantz and Guildenstern Are Dead*, and Moon and Birdboot are both drama critics, actors, and victims in *The Real Inspector Hound*.

One of the most successful burlesques in English is Beaumont and Fletcher's *The Knight of the Burning Pestle* (1607), in which romantic-heroic themes are systematically devalued by the citizen and his wife and their apprentice Rafe, who plays a wide variety of elevated roles in his interpolated play (or collection of scenes from the popular, middle-class drama of the period). The humor turns on the incongruity of subject and style. Thus Rafe, in leaving Pompiona, the princess of Cracovia, proffers tips all around: "And last, fair lady, there is for yourself / Threepence to buy you pins at Bumbo Fair." The ease with which these sums are offered undercuts all heroic pretensions, just as Humphrey in wooing Luce, the merchant's daughter, presents a pair of gloves whose cost he is not at all ashamed of:

> *If you desire the price, shoot from your eye*
> *A beam to this place, and you shall espy*
> *"F S," which is to say, my sweetest honey,*
> *They cost me three and twopence, or no money.*

The price code, "F S," is a touching reminder of commercial life, which lies just beneath the romantic surface of the play.

Similarly, Humphrey's thrifty enumeration neutralizes the romantic ardor of the original in this parody of *Romeo and Juliet*: "Good night, twenty good nights, and twenty more, / And twenty more good nights—that makes threescore!" The burlesque depends on the wide gap between the intended meaning and the vehicle in which it is expressed; the abrupt contrast between grand subject and ignoble style marks the omnipresence of bathos in this kind of writing. If Beaumont and Fletcher really meant to hold the citizens and their values up to scorn before the elite audience of the private theater, they failed dismally, since the middle-class world of the play is so endearing, so charming, and so wittily conceived. We grow especially fond of the Citizen's Wife, who is constantly expressing an unlimited compassion and tenderness for both the actors and the audience. She makes no distinction between the fictive world of the play and the real world of the playhouse, and she is equally at ease in both.

Rafe is reserved for special effects of grandiloquence and magniloquence, as he enters portentously for his death speech *"with a forked arrow through his head."* Beaumont and Fletcher make large demands on our ability to recognize allusions, since the speech begins with a parody of Kyd's *The Spanish Tragedy* (1587), probably the most parodied play of its time:

> *When I was mortal, this my costive [constipated] corpse*
> *Did lap up figs and raisins in the Strand [a commercial street in*
> *   London],*
> *Where sitting, I espied a lovely dame,*

> *Whose master wrought with lingel [waxed thread] and with awl,*
> *And underground he vampied [patched] many a boot.*

The heroic sentiments are firmly attached to a context of shoemaking (as in Dekker's *Shoemaker's Holiday*), and despite his romantic adventures, Ralph remains faithful to his "black-thumbed maid, Susan." He dies with an heroic vaunt: "I die! Fly, fly, my soul, to Grocers' Hall / O, O, O, etc." Curiously enough, these are the same "O" groans with which Hamlet and Lear expire, but which are always omitted in modern editions. To modern ears, they seem to parody a death where flocks of angels sing the departed soul to its rest.

The Restoration vogue for high-flown, heroic tragedy stimulated Buckingham's burlesque, *The Rehearsal* (1671), which pokes fun at the pretentious nonsense of its playwright-hero, Bayes, who is modeled on Dryden. The play is delightfully literary in its assumptions and practice. Aside from specific satire and ridicule, it is one of our earliest examples of metadrama, since its real subject is the art of writing heroic tragedy. By a nice paradoxical turn, the aspirations of Bayes to high tragedy provide a perfect subject for comedy. There is no way that this formula could be reversed and a comic subject be made to generate tragedy.

One of Buckingham's techniques is to literalize some of the favorite themes of heroic tragedy. Thus, the omnipresent conflict between Love and Honor is represented by two boots, which Volscius cannot make up his mind either to put on or to put off. His lucid debate with himself parodies the reflective soliloquy of the tragic hero, faced with a difficult decision:

> *My Legs, the Emblem of my various thought,*
> *Shew to what sad distraction I am brought.*
> *Sometimes with stubborn Honour, like this Boot,*
> *My mind is guarded, and resolv'd: to do't:*
> *Sometimes, again, that very mind, by Love*
> *Disarmed, like this other Leg does prove.*
> *Shall I to Honour or to Love give way?*
> *Go on, cries Honour; tender Love saies, nay:*

Honour, aloud, commands, pluck both Boots on;
But softer Love does whisper put on none.

The problem is insoluble for Volscius, and he *"Goes out hopping with
one Boot on, and the other off."* *The Rehearsal* is so effective because
Buckingham is well acquainted with the plays on which his burlesque is based. He is secure enough in his parody to consistently
underplay any broad and obvious touches.

We are constantly made to admire the brilliance of Buckingham's
own writing, especially when he is mocking the high poetic sensibility. His couplets on the boar and sow are offered as "one of the
most delicate dainty *Simile's* in the whole world":

'Tis an allusion to love.
So Boar and Sow, when any storm is nigh,
Snuff up, and smell it gath'ring in the Sky;
Boar beckons Sow to trot in Chestnut Groves,
And there consummate their unfinish'd Loves:
Pensive in mud they wallow all alone,
And snore and gruntle to each others moan.

The gross sexuality of the final couplet is masked by the refinement
of the style.

The rhetoric is consciously out of phase with the subject; it is, in
fact, completely autonomous, because, as Bayes points out, "That's
a general Rule, you must ever make a *simile*, when you are sur-
pris'd; 'tis the new way of writing." *The Rehearsal* is as much a burlesque of the art of criticism as of the art of heroic tragedy, since it
echoes catch-phrases of the critical controversies of the day. Johnson, for example, reports that "the new kind of Wits" define the
function of poetry as "to elevate and surprise," which means
"Fighting, Loving, Sleeping, Rhyming, Dying, Dancing, Singing,
Crying; and every thing, but thinking and Sence." As Bayes puts it
later: "the chief Art in Poetry is to elevate your expectation, and
then bring you off some extraordinary way." Buckingham is ridi-
culing an excessive refinement and artificiality in manners as well
as in the theater. Social and literary criteria flow together.

None of the other plays in Simon Trussler's fine anthology, *Bur-*

lesque Plays of the Eighteenth Century, matches the ease and grace of *The Rehearsal*. Fielding's *Tom Thumb* (1730) is a notable example of burlesque wit, but not as subtle and as various as *The Rehearsal*; *Tom Thumb* is only a brief afterpiece to a full-length play. Fielding's skill lies in his exploitation of bathos, which Trussler defines as "a toppling from the lofty to the ludicrous." The great Shakespearean blank-verse tragedies of the previous century are mercilessly pilloried by the diminutive and ridiculous characters. As the beautiful princess Huncamunca puts her plight, echoing *Romeo and Juliet*, "O, *Tom Thumb! Tom Thumb!* wherefore art thou *Tom Thumb?*"

Some of the dialogue features old-fashioned comic routines. Thus, when Tom Thumb in love rapturously exclaims: "I know not where, nor how, nor what I am, / I'm so transported, I have lost my self," Huncamunca chooses to literalize his metaphor: "Forbid it, all the Stars; for you're so small, / That were you lost, you'd find your self no more." This is not exactly delicate or subtle, and the King's wedding blessing gets caught up in a grotesque Homeric simile:

> *Long may ye live, and love, and propagate,*
> *'Till the whole Land be peopled with* Tom Thumbs.
> *So when the* Cheshire-*Cheese a Maggot breeds,*
> *Another and another still succeeds;*
> *By thousands and ten thousands they encrease,*
> *Till one continu'd Maggot fills the rotten Cheese.*

This hyperbolic extravagance is typical of the play, which is an extended exercise in bad taste not unlike the Marx Brothers, who had a special genius for burlesque, as in their musical-comedy spoof of academic life at the beginning of *Horse Feathers* (see Figure 10).

Sheridan's *The Critic* (1779) is a burlesque only in the parts dealing with Puff's Elizabethan play, *The Spanish Armada*. It looks as if Sheridan had been reading Shakespeare closely, because *The Critic* so specifically echoes Shakespearean lines. Tilburina's mad speech, for example, collects bits and pieces from Ophelia's part in *Hamlet* (as well as other scraps from *Hamlet*, Webster's *The White Devil*, and Marlowe's *Tamburlaine, Part II*):

Figure 10. In a Burlesque, Musical-Comedy Setting, Groucho Marx as Professor Wagstaff Is Installed as President of Huxley College (*Horse Feathers,* Paramount, 1932); *The Museum of Modern Art / Film Stills Archive.*

The wind whistles—the moon rises—see,
They have killed my squirrel in his cage!
Is this a grasshopper!—Ha! No, it is my
Whiskerandos [her dead lover]—you shall not keep him—
I know you have him in your pocket—
An oyster may be crossed in love!—Who says
A whale's a bird?—Ha! did you call, my love?
—He's here! He's here!—He's everywhere!
Ah me! He's nowhere!

Sheridan had a marvelous ear for the inflated absurdities of Elizabethan tragedy, and his burlesque is rollicking good fun that makes few demands on the audience, either critical or stylistic.

Sheridan's nostalgic mood is always genial and good-humored, as in his glance at plagiarism. Puff's "mysterious yeoman," a beefeater in uniform, enters and at once declares: "Perdition catch my soul, but I do love thee." Othello's line is politely accepted by the well-mannered auditors:

> *SNEER:* Haven't I heard that line before?
> *PUFF.* No, I fancy not. Where, pray?
> *DANGLE.* Yes, I think there is something like it in *Othello.*
> *PUFF.* Gad! now you put me in mind on't, I believe there is; but that's of no consequence—all that can be said is, that two people happened to hit on the same thought—and Shakespeare made use of it first, that's all.

How gracious the humor is! Sheridan's Puff is a harmless, entertaining creature, much like the Citizens and Rafe in *The Knight of the Burning Pestle*, and his burlesque has none of the satirical bite of *The Rehearsal* and *Tom Thumb.* Burlesque as a dramatic form lends itself better to high spirits and good fun than to acrimonious literary and critical controversy. Skill in parody produces bravura passages to be admired and laughed at. In some sense, the parody tries to replace the original by making its own art so convincingly superior.

In comedy of manners, the wits are arbiters of good taste, while the butts are awkward, stiff, pretentious, and social misfits.

In comedy of manners, the wits make the rules and define the criteria by which persons are judged either not to qualify as wits or to be outside the system entirely. By definition, the audience agrees with the wits, who represent a fixed set of attitudes and mores.

The comedy of manners formula is therefore very simple: every-thing that violates social norms and expectations is subject to ridi-cule. By convention, the audience identifies with the wits on stage, even though they are obviously literary creations.

The wits are cool, detached, self-assured, hedonistic, and mali-cious, whereas the butts are clumsy, blunt, foppish, and full of self-love. The wits are fine speakers, resourceful, inventive, lovers—and quoters—of poetry, but the poor butts are gross in their intellect, crude in speech and sensibility, and totally without the deftness and agility of mind needed to succeed in social life. This broad dichotomy, intentionally simplified and schematized, lies at the heart of the comedy of manners, in which the audience can take sides and laugh at its own much-satirized foibles. Since comedy of manners is so social, it offers comic purgation (as well as specific instruction) for those who wear the wrong clothes, buy at the wrong shops, are clumsy in love, and are otherwise crude and materialistic in their lifestyle.

This kind of comedy has flourished at periods when audiences have been strongly homogeneous and could give their spontaneous approval to the sentiments of the characters on stage. Comedy of manners is particularly associated with an aristocratic or upper-class audience as opposed to a popular and middle-class public, who would be more inclined to morals than manners and to a senti-mental and didactic drama. By the 1630s in England, during the reign of Charles I, there was a much sharper division between upper classes and court party, who patronized the theaters, and the middle and lower classes, who didn't.

In a play like James Shirley's *The Lady of Pleasure* (1635), the com-edy of manners formulas of the Restoration (1660 to about 1700) are already clearly evident. Everything turns on the distinction be-tween good and bad taste. Thus, there are two ladies of pleasure, one false and one authentic. Aretina, the wife of Sir Thomas Born-well, does everything wrong. She gambles, she dissipates her es-tate, she engages in meaningless flirtations, and even commits the unpardonable sin of buying the services of a ridiculous fop, Alex-ander Kickshaw, who boasts of his new-found luck as kept man. Celestina, the young widow, is just the opposite of Aretina. She is always wonderfully in control, and even though she pursues her pleasure and advantage in this world, she does it with notable charm and control. She is always a lady and a winner.

Celestina's opening scene with her steward is a splendid example of how the comedy of manners could sometimes undertake to educate its audiences in the specifics of good taste. Celestina is roundly rebuking her steward for trying to save money, for buying "cheap stuff" that will not do credit to a great lady of pleasure. The dialogue gets technical in places, and we need footnotes to distinguish, for example, between noble and ignoble fabrics. Thus, Celestina wants the inside of her coach to be upholstered with "crimson plush," but the bungling and parsimonious steward has had it done in "crimson camel plush." The mistress vents her snobbish fury on such outrageous economy:

> *Ten thousand moths consume't! Shall I ride through*
> *The streets in penance, wrapp'd up in haircloth?*
> *Sell't to an alderman; 't will serve his wife*
> *To go a-feasting to their country-house,*
> *Or fetch a merchant's nurse-child, and come home*
> *Laden with fruit and cheese-cakes. I despise it! (1.2.29–34)*

It then turns out that the ornamental nails are "single gilt" and not "double gilt," and Celestina is once more in a fury:

> *The nails not double gilt! To market wo't? [Will you go to*
> *market in it?]*
> *'T will hackney out to Mile End [training grounds for Lon-*
> *don militia and place of fairs and shows], or convey*
> *Your city tumblers [prostitutes] to be drunk with cream*
> *And prunes at Islington [a place of assignation outside*
> *London]. (1.2.41–44)*

Celestina is determined to "spare no cost / That may engage all generous report / To trumpet forth my bounty and my bravery [showy grandeur]" (1.2.81–83). She wisely invests her money to catch a husband, whereas Aretina is foolish in everything she does and is only rescued from ruin at the last moment by her husband's clever device.

Restoration comedy of manners follows directly from these Caroline examples. In *The Man of Mode* (1676) by George Etherege, everyone makes fun of Sir Fopling Flutter, a frenchified dandy who carries refined taste to a ridiculous extreme. His first appearance in the play in Act III, Scene ii is marked almost entirely by talk of the latest fashions, and he sets himself out as a clothed object to be admired rather than as a human being:

> *SIR FOPLING.* A slight suit I made to appear in at my first arrival—not worthy your consideration, ladies.
> *DORIMANT.* The pantaloon is very well mounted.
> *SIR FOPLING.* The tassels are new and pretty.
> *MEDLEY.* I never saw a coat better cut.
> *SIR FOPLING.* It makes me show long-waisted, and I think slender.
> *DORIMANT.* That's the shape our ladies dote on.
> *MEDLEY.* Your breech, though, is a handful too high, in my eye, Sir Fopling.
> *SIR FOPLING.* Peace, Medley, I have wished it lower a thousand times; but a pox on't, 'twill not be! (3.2.190–200)

The dialogue soon degenerates into a remarkable passage that merely catalogues the most fashionable merchants of Paris:

> *LADY TOWNLEY.* The suit?
> *SIR FOPLING.* Barroy.
> *EMILIA.* The garniture?
> *SIR FOPLING.* Le Gras.
> *MEDLEY.* The shoes?
> *SIR FOPLING.* Piccar.
> *DORIMANT.* The periwig?
> *SIR FOPLING.* Chedreux.
> *LADY TOWNLEY. EMILIA.* The gloves?
> *SIR FOPLING.* Orangerie. You know the smell, ladies.
> (3.2.206–15)

This is pure snobbery, but of course it is used to show that Sir Fopling Flutter is a fool; all of the wits in the play are properly aristocratic and nonchalant about their clothes. This catechism of smart shops is a characteristic piece of dialogue, since it assumes that the audience will immediately recognize and approve of the names. And for those who might miss a name or two, it is appropriate for them to make a quiet note in their memoranda books.

It would be a mistake to think of the comedy of manners as only an expression of social snobbery, although that aspect colors our sense of the in-group and the out-group. But the standards for the in-group are incomparably higher. Beginning with the right clothes and an infallible sense of the social occasion, the true wit moves on to an intuition for the appropriate gesture and the right word. The final criteria for wit are intellectual poise, mental agility, skill at repartee, epigrammatic brilliance, and a genuis for *le mot juste*, so that the wit is ultimately judged by aesthetic standards that give the illusion of being social standards. As Dryden understood in his mock-heroic poem, *Mac Flecknoe* (1682), and Pope in his mock-epic, *The Dunciad* (1728), the one unforgivable offense against manners is dullness. In "dull" are comprehended all the vices and pretensions of bad manners and false society.

The aesthetic dimension of wit is beautifully illustrated by Congreve's *The Way of the World*, which, in 1700, was already looking back nostalgically at the sort of Restoration comedy of manners that had virtually disappeared. Millamant is the most brilliant of Restoration heroines, and she is the true heir of Shakespeare's vivacious and outrageously witty women (like Rosalind in *As You Like It*, Beatrice in *Much Ado About Nothing*, and even Juliet in *Romeo and Juliet*). Millamant has been matched with the boorish, but good-natured Sir Wilfull Witwoud. In their awkward wooing scene, Millamant's quotation from John Suckling, a poet of the seventeenth century, is totally misunderstood:

> MILLAMANT. (*repeating*) I swear it [my heart] will not do its part,
> Though thou dost thine, employ'st thy power and art.
> Natural, easy Suckling!
> SIR WILFUL. Anan? Suckling? No such suckling neither, cousin, nor stripling; I thank heaven, I'm no minor.
> MILLAMANT. Ah, rustic! ruder than Gothic! (IV, 90–95)

Millamant is dismayed by Witwoud's gross ignorance of poetry (as if he might have said "Milton who?"), but when Mirabell enters, he is able to complete her couplet (this time from a poem by Edmund Waller, a contemporary poet who died in 1687):

MILLAMANT. Like Phoebus sung the no less amorous boy.
MIRABELL. Like Daphne she, as lovely and as coy.
(IV, 133–34)

This is the moment we have been waiting for: the sign that Mirabell has finally won Millamant, and they move from the couplet directly into their wonderfully satiric stipulation of the marriage articles. Mirabell triumphs by his wit; he is the only man worthy of Millamant.

Oscar Wilde's play, *The Importance of Being Earnest* (1895), revives the comedy of manners format of the Restoration, but Wilde is much more openly satirical of middle-class values and moral assumptions. The characters are mostly idle rich (or servant parodies of the idle rich), who spend their time in pursuing ladies and other associated pleasures. It is all very upper-class British, but the aristocratic characters themselves think their way of life absurd and only continue in it to trick the middle class with patently false illusions. "Earnestness" in all of its forms, including the name Ernest, is mercilessly ridiculed. All the characters flourish in a purely aesthetic and nonmoral dimension, where epigrammatic wit is the only value in an otherwise tawdry and meaningless existence. When Jack reveals the melodramatic details of his parentage —found in a hand-bag in the cloak-room at Victoria Station—Lady Bracknell rises to her greatest heights of mock-indignation: "To be born, or at any rate bred, in a hand-bag, whether it had handles or not, seems to me to display a contempt for the ordinary decencies of family life that reminds one of the worst excesses of the French Revolution."

"Whether it had handles or not" is splendidly irrelevant, matched only by Lady Bracknell's withering pun: "Until yesterday I had no idea that there were any families or persons whose origin was a Terminus." All of these absurdities are spoken with perfect *froideur* and haughtiness, so that Wilde's comedy of manners balances on the edge of high farce. Lady Bracknell draws tremendous vitality from being so thoroughly conceived as a social type rather than a carefully developed, psychologically shaded character. Her mad one-dimensionality endows her with comic energy, and her furious social pronouncements are every bit as good as we anticipate: "You can hardly imagine that I and Lord Bracknell would dream of allowing our only daughter—a girl brought up with the utmost care—to marry into a cloak-room, and form an alliance with a parcel. Good morning, Mr. Worthing!"

So Jack must now clear up the mystery of his origins, and the play proceeds with an abundance of melodramatic detail, including a "three-volume novel of more than usually revolting sentimentality" left in a pram by Miss Prism, the governess. The swirling plot becomes a vehicle for making social and aesthetic points, and the triumph of wit becomes a mock-justification for upper-class values. The wits in the comedy of manners are always ironically conceived, and their function is to mock the foibles of others rather than to set up their own manners as a criterion of value. Good taste is the intuitive grace of all wits, but it is never insisted on with any tedious particularity. Good taste and facility in speech come naturally to those who deprecate their own gifts—of which an amused self-deprecation is one of the chief.

Satiric comedy seeks to display and control its villain-heroes.

The villain-hero in comedy is an anomalous figure, since the villain has natural affinities with wrongdoing and evil, which are the proper subjects of tragedy. The villain-hero in comedy is doomed to failure from the start. He energizes the play with his vigorous and relentless pursuit of the wrong objectives, but he is always contained by the comic action. At the end, he is either reconciled to the new society of the young and pure in heart (who marry or are about to marry), or is expelled from it—left behind, as Caliban is on the island of *The Tempest*, or Jaques in the Forest of Arden (incidentally, the family name of Shakespeare's mother) in *As You Like*

It. Malvolio's claims in *Twelfth Night* about being revenged on the whole pack of plotters and practical jokers are not meant to be taken seriously and certainly do not direly predict the Puritan Revolution, as some high-minded critics would have it.

Shylock is the most disturbing of the villain-heroes in comedy, since *The Merchant of Venice* finds it difficult to reconcile the realistic, commercial world of Venice with the romantic, folktale, celebratory world of Belmont. Does Shylock really have the tragic overtones that have been so strongly emphasized in the theatrical tradition? To play Shylock as a tragic hero incongruously caught up in a comic action profoundly misunderstands the satiric comedy of *The Merchant of Venice*, just as a tragic Malvolio is also grotesquely out of place in *Twelfth Night*. There is no tragic context in either *The Merchant of Venice* or *Twelfth Night* to support this interpretation. Both Shylock and Malvolio are isolated figures out of keeping with the world of the play.

As satirical commentator, Shylock scores remarkably good points against the hypocrisy of the Christian society from which he has been excluded. It is quite clearly a slave-owning society, and Shylock is shrewd enough to fight his opponents with their own legalistic, property-oriented morality:

> *You have among you many a purchased slave,*
> *Which like your asses and your dogs and mules*
> *You use in abject and in slavish parts,*
> *Because you bought them. Shall I say to you,*
> *"Let them be free! Marry them to your heirs!*
> *Why sweat they under burdens? Let their beds*
> *Be made as soft as yours, and let their palates*
> *Be seasoned with such viands"? You will answer,*
> *"The slaves are ours." So do I answer you:*
> *The pound of flesh which I demand of him*
> *Is dearly bought, is mine, and I will have it.*
> *If you deny me, fie upon your law!* (4.1.90–101)

There is an unctuous sarcasm in the mock-liberal speech Shylock arrogates to himself. He is a master of heavy innuendo and self-conscious gloating, but he is still extraordinarily perceptive in his paradoxes of liberty and law. He is a master of satire just because he knows so well how to embarrass his auditors—to turn the tables on their shallow rectitude.

In his first encounter with Antonio, Shylock sardonically puts Antonio in his place:

> *You call me misbeliever, cutthroat dog,*
> *And spet upon my Jewish gaberdine,*
> *And all for use of that which is mine own.*
> *Well then, it now appears you need my help.*
> *Go to, then. You come to me and you say,*
> *"Shylock, we would have moneys"—you say so,*
> *You that did void your rheum [spit] upon my beard*
> *And foot me as you spurn a stranger cur*
> *Over your threshold! Moneys is your suit.*
> *What should I say to you? Should I not say,*
> *"Hath a dog money? Is it possible*
> *A cur can lend three thousand ducats?"* (1.3.108–19)

This is a very histrionic speech, and Shylock is enjoying his role as victim-turned-benefactor. No doubt that he is right in feeling unjustly abused, but how self-righteous he is with his venomous interrogations. It is too much: comic hyperbole, overreaching, an excess of rubbing it in and malevolent zeal.

We are not meant to take Shylock at face value as a spokesman for oppressed strangers or outsiders. All of his excellent debater's points are undercut by his own satirical malice, and we recall the popular (but false) derivation of "satire" from "satyr," a rough, gross, coarse, violent woodland deity, half-man, half-beast, associated with Dionysus/Bacchus. Shylock lacks tragic dignity and stature; he is a snarling, wheedling, ill-tempered satirist, who is permanently excluded from the society of both Venice and Belmont, and who can only rail in the malicious spirit of Thersites in *Troilus and Cressida* and Timon and Apemantus in *Timon of Athens*. The bitter, misanthropic satirists may speak a cunning truth—and they are usually more perceptive and intelligent than good-spirited persons—but they are by no means the moral centers of their plays. The truth lies elsewhere.

Satiric comedy unleashes tremendous energies that are only partly controlled by the dramatic action. Shylock on stage is a large and exciting figure, who gives *The Merchant of Venice* a sharpness and acuity of interest that could not have been derived from strictly romantic sources. It is hard comedy, comedy with an edge, as Molière understood it in plays like *The Misanthrope* (1666), *Tartuffe* (1667), and *The Miser* (1668). Molière knew how to animate these dangerous and explosive materials in a completely believable, natural, and witty action. The social norms which measure and contain the satirist's outrage are more rigidly defined in Molière than in Shakespeare, which gives his comedy greater moral lucidity. There is less ambivalence than there is in Shakespeare, although *The Misanthrope* lends itself to romantic and sentimental distortion by critics.

The point in that play, as in all satiric comedy, is that truth-speaking should not be confused with truth. Alceste's extraordinary insight into the moral pretense and hypocrisy of his society—its false gestures, its emptiness, its hedonism, its crassness, and its self-serving materialism—does not excuse his own surliness, harshness, and want of good manners. He is as egotistical and exhibitionistic as the objects of his satire, and Célimène is right to refuse his very conditional ardors. His self-imposed exile at the end of the play is a self-imposed punishment for his lack of compassion and sympathy for his fellow human beings. All of this undercutting of Alceste as a character and as a human being is not, of course, meant to deny the aptness and rightness of his satirical thrusts.

It is highly dramatic to see Alceste in action, lashing out at the petty vanities and pretentious vices of the world, but the norms of the play seem to rest with more limited, more moderate, and more commonsensical characters such as Philinte, Alceste's friend. In the debate between them which opens the play, Philinte is the spokesman for an ironic, tempered view of human foibles: "I take, with equanimity, men as they are; I accustom my spirit to accept what they do . . ."; "Perfect reason avoids all extremities"; "Let's show a little gracious understanding of human nature." Alceste, in his uncompromising fury, is himself becoming an object of ridicule, but his wildness is fascinating to observe. With demonic energy, he attacks false values and sets up ideals of human probity and sincerity that no one, least of all himself, can possibly fulfill.

There is an element of futile grandeur in the following statement of principle: "I want men to be men, and in every encounter, what is really in our hearts should show itself in our conversation. Whoever speaks and whatever our feelings are should never be masked under a show of foolish compliments." I am translating the formal French couplets freely in order to catch the outrageous high-mindedness of Alceste's program for mankind. Even in his courtship of Célimène, a satirical spirit marvelously well suited for him, Alceste makes demands that cannot possibly be met. His irritating jealousy is really an expression of his own narrow possessiveness and self-concern, as Célimène so well understands when she attempts to calm his pointless rage in Act IV, Scene iii: "Really, you are a madman in your jealous fit, and you don't deserve the love I have for you. I would certainly like to know what could stop me from stooping, for your sake, to the baseness of feigning, or why, if my heart were inclined a different way, I shouldn't tell it to you with all sincerity." Alceste is so preoccupied with dishonesty that he doesn't allow for spontaneously good-hearted impulses in others. He is himself incapable of love, and his self-exile from human society comes as no surprise at the end of play. He is not properly human.

Molière's *Misanthrope* takes satire as far as it will go in the direction of uncompromising attack on the frailties of human reason and the preposterousness of our pretended virtue, but Alceste is deeply undercut by his own rigorous "Satire Against Mankind" (as the Earl of Rochester called his own adaptation of Juvenal). It is not so farfetched to suggest a link between characters such as Alceste and Tartuffe—not that Alceste is in any way an oily hypocrite like Tartuffe, but both are satirical extremes and both are separated from ordinary human norms. Tartuffe is self-consciously an actor in a human comedy he himself stages and manipulates, but Alceste, too, in his abandonment of good sense and sweet reasonableness, is consciously histrionic. It is this element of calculation that separates both characters from tragedy. Alceste and Tartuffe are alien figures in their respective plays. Despite their successes—and Tartuffe comes dangerously close to being a total winner—they are set firmly in a social context hostile to their interests. The world of the play is the world of comedy: vain social types in *The Misanthrope*, young lovers and a witty servant (Dorine) in *Tartuffe*. Alceste and

Tartuffe violate the comic norms of their plays, yet, despite that, it is remarkable how influential and successful they become. Their power is a tribute to the force of satire, which is needed to correct the complacency, self-satisfaction, and smug self-assurance of the comic society of the play.

The Misanthrope and *Tartuffe* are, of course, very different kinds of plays. Tartuffe is a villain-hero, who becomes positively menacing in the course of the play—the more menacing, the more attractive dramatically; that is, he fascinates us by his amazing and unaccountable success, twisting each adverse revelation to his own benefit. The play turns, however, not on Tartuffe's evil (as it would in tragedy), but on Orgon's incredible blindness. As we expect in comedy, the peripeteia (or change in fortune) is managed swiftly and effortlessly and without any moral involvement: the husband concealed under the table finally has the ocular and aural proof he needs to be convinced that Tartuffe has designs on his wife.

While exploding religious hypocrisy, Tartuffe also serves to complete Orgon's education and, in some fashion, to humanize him. In a minor way, the same reformation is also effected for Madame Pernelle, Orgon's stiff-necked, strait-laced, and authoritarian mother. Tartuffe's evil is always neutralized by the comic context, which asserts the values of normal, fallible, concupiscent human beings. It is therefore pure self-indulgence to speak of the play as a tragicomedy or dark comedy, because we are never allowed to believe that Tartuffe can really triumph. There is nothing in the play to support a comparison of Tartuffe and Shakespeare's Iago. Orgon is terribly slow to realize what is happening, but he never undergoes the spiritual transformation of Othello.

Tartuffe is such a satisfying part for an actor because Molière has such a keen sense of comic artifice. Tartuffe doesn't appear until more than a third of the play is over; by that point we are almost over-ready for his smooth and facile role-playing. The character is conceived broadly, but there are a great many subtle touches by which his blatant hypocrisy is expressed. His attempt to seduce Elmire, the warm and gracious wife of Orgon, is laced with jesuitical casuistry that will at once flatter her and satisfy her religious scruples: "Ah, to be religious doesn't make me any less a man, and when one sees your divine attractions, a heart lets itself be caught up and doesn't reason. I know that this kind of talk from me appears strange, but, madame, after all, I am no angel." We admire Tartuffe because he speaks so well, and his malevolence is mitigated by his comic inventiveness. He is always resourceful, imaginative, and never at a loss for words.

We might even go so far as to say that Tartuffe is lovable, in the sense that we love to hear him talk and that we grow impatient when he is not on stage. He is so beautifully adaptable to circumstance that he can only exist because of the foolish gullibility and culpability of others. There is no doubt that he has a hard and vicious edge, but this energizes the comedy rather than detracts from it. Tartuffe sets in motion Dorine, the witty servant in the tradition of Plautus, and she is a more than worthy antagonist in a debate that can have only one conclusion. The good people of the play all owe their existence to Tartuffe, who has such abundant vitality that he requires a whole family of related characters to effect his comeuppance.

Harpagon in *The Miser* is lovable in a simpler and more direct sense. Although his comic villainy is plain to all, he seems much more an eccentric, cantankerous old gentleman than a serious moral threat to his son and daughter. Are stinginess and miserliness really being satirized in this play, as the ostensible subject would suggest, or is the play rather a vehicle for the display of comic niggardliness and the traditional buffoonery of the old father as rival in love to his young son? I think there is no way of answering this question, since satire always maintains this double perspective of subject and object. In other words, although the subject of the play may be the repulsion of miserly attitudes, the object of the play is to display them so fully as to convince us of the need to purge them. Harpagon has a certain preposterous attraction that the blander persons in the play lack. He is devious and various and relies on the resources of comic invention.

His grotesque lamentations in Act IV, Scene vii, for his lost "cassette" (or strongbox) echo Shylock's indiscriminate mingling of his ducats and his daughter: "Stop! (*To himself, taking himself by the arm*) Give me back my money, rogue. . . . Ah! It's me! My mind is troubled, and I don't know where I am, who I am, and what I'm doing. Alas! my poor money! my poor money! my dear friend! I have been deprived of you, and since you have been taken away from me, I have lost my support, my consolation, my joy. Everything is finished for me and I have nothing more to do in the world. Without you it is impossible for me to live." The personification of the money as a lost friend or lost mistress is absurdly touching, and the soliloquy ends with the same extravagant impulse: "I want to hang the whole world, and if I don't recover my money, I will hang myself afterward." This clown's routine of Harpagon endears him to the audience, to whom he has been playing. We are convinced that his hard-heartedness to his children is the merest affectation of a very foolish, fond old man, who has all the traditional weaknesses of the *senex* of Roman comedy. At the end of the play, he actually does trade off the chance to marry the young and luscious Mariane for the return of his "cassette"—with a new suit thrown in for lagniappe.

The geniality of satirical comedy is probably best illustrated by the plays of George Bernard Shaw, who found it difficult to move from his comedy of manners settings to the world of ideas and values. Shaw had such an extraordinary genius for the exact social gesture that it becomes almost impossible to separate the gesture from the larger meaning it is intended to express. In *Major Barbara* (1905), for example, the villain-hero is Andrew Undershaft, a munitions manufacturer, who manages to convert his daughter, Barbara, a major in the Salvation Army, from her religious commitments, which are seen to be as shallow and hypocritical as those in *Tartuffe*. Undershaft suavely turns Christian morality inside out— our worst crime is poverty—and at the very moment of his triumph over Barbara he slyly alludes to Shakespeare's Shylock: "My ducats and my daughter!" Undershaft's ducats have conquered *his* daughter.

It's difficult to take Shaw's satire seriously, since it leaves itself open to further satire on the utopian vision that will correct the present evils. Thus Undershaft in his factory-town, model community extols the virtues of material comfort and well-being over those of abstract Christian morality: "Cleanliness and respectability do not need justification, Barbara: they justify themselves. I see no darkness here, no dreadfulness. In your Salvation shelter I saw

poverty, misery, cold and hunger. You gave them bread and trea-
cle and dreams of heaven. I give from thirty shillings a week to
twelve thousand a year. They find their own dreams; but I look
after the drainage." The saving grace of the play is that Shaw is
constantly poking fun at his moralizing characters. In *Major Barbara*, Undershaft's aristocratic wife, Lady Britomart, maintains her
uncommitted and non-ideological skepticism throughout. Like
Lady Bracknell in *The Importance of Being Earnest*, she is never converted to or from anything, and we are cheerfully inclined to agree
with her when she says curtly to her husband: "Your ideas are nonsense. You got on because you were selfish and unscrupulous."
Shaw solves the problem of his satire by constantly deflating it.

Festive comedy vanquishes all obstructions and asserts a hedonistic, holiday, carnival spirit.

The term "festive comedy" is coming into general use to describe
ritualistic, celebratory comedy, especially plays associated with
popular festivals and holidays. C. L. Barber's book, *Shakespeare's
Festive Comedy* (1959), was influential in showing the relation of
Shakespeare's comedies to the folk customs and social institutions
of his time, and Mikhail Bakhtin's massive study, *Rabelais and His
World* (1968), connects Rabelais with ancient and medieval traditions of holiday merrymaking and earthy humor arising from food
and drink, sex, and bodily functions. We have already spoken
about the assumptions of festive comedy in the section on comic
endings: the comic structure moves inexorably toward the fulfillment of the marriage feast, with its drinking, dancing, revelry, sexual license, and promise of offspring. In festive comedy proper, the
festive mood penetrates all aspects of the play world and not just
the ending. The daily, workaday world is banished or confuted almost from the beginning, and a different set of rules applies.

Aristophanes is essential for understanding festive plays, since he
is our chief representative of Old Comedy. Unlike the New Comedy of Plautus and Terence, Old Comedy has much less interest in

plot and sexual intrigue. Its characters are less rigorously defined in their prescriptive roles, and it is a looser form, with more resemblances to musical comedy or to a series of related skits in a revue than to situation comedy. In a typical play of Aristophanes, two large ideas are set into conflict with each other: peace versus war, youth versus age, Aeschylus versus Euripides, right reason versus wrong reason. At the center of the play is the *agon*, or debate, in which the idea favored by the playwright is made to prevail.

The characters are usually ordinary, unheroic Athenians, who have some wild idea or scheme they are promoting. Lysistrata, who leads the women's sex strike, has no special distinction before the play begins. Similarly, Pisthetairos, who establishes the kingdom of the birds in *The Birds*, begins as only another discontented Athenian who wants to do something about the status quo. Dikaiopolis in *The Acharnians* is "*a disconsolate, ragged old farmer who has been forced into Athens to do sentry duty*"; there is no way of predicting that he will make a separate peace with the Spartans and become a folk hero. None of Aristophanes' heroes has any heroic potential. The choruses are also supremely unheroic. They literally express community standards without any special moral commitment, political enlightenment, or rhetorical skill. In *The Wasps*, the chorus consists of a pack of unsavory, prejudiced, and litigious old men costumed as wasps and with the capacity to sting. Decrepit, impotent, and ridiculous old men form the chorus in *Lysistrata*. In *The Birds*, the chorus are birds, some ridiculously and flamboyantly costumed; the entrance of the chorus is deliberately spaced out to make a big "production number."

Aristophanes is not an esoteric, intellectual playwright, and the new colloquial, jazzy translations in the Mentor Books series (edited by William Arrowsmith) give the impression of a writer very much in tune with the popular idiom. Aristophanes' great theme is war and peace. Living in the late fifth century B.C. at a time of almost constant warfare between Athens and Sparta—the Peloponnesian War makes the same frustrating and hopeless impression as the Thirty Years' War that lies behind Brecht's *Mother Courage*—Aristophanes protests the war, on humanistic grounds, as an offense against human dignity and the human spirit. The continued, meaningless war blocks all the hedonistic values connected not just with peace, but with the enjoyment of life. Aristophanes is imaginatively projecting what it would be like to be at peace again, and his plays often take the form of wish-fulfillment fantasies.

The point about Lysistrata is not that she is some sex-crazed nymphomaniac intent on the ultimate political striptease. She is an ordinary housewife and mother, but she is now desperate. Her sex strike to force an end to the war is the act of an inspired, demonic person who not only has no other possibility for active participation in the government of Athens, but also has nothing to lose. She is a nonpolitical person who has had enough. Her organization of the women of Greece is a mad, frenzied act, a hare-brained scheme no one takes seriously until it is wildly successful. The feminist assertions in the play are not part of any ideological program on Aristophanes' part—there is good reason to believe that he was strongly conservative in his politics—but an expression of the vivacious, energetic, heady, and liberating mood of the play.

Festive comedy affirms the dreamlike principle that all things are possible—at least at this special, inspired moment of the play and for a limited time only. In the splendid sex scene between Myrrhine and her tumescent husband, Kinesias, he will promise her anything in order to make love to her, but Myrrhine, a good patriot, teases and frustrates him at the same time. She is also, of course, teasing and frustrating herself, and at one point in the play, when things are looking bleak for Lysistrata and her girls, she admits the truth: "we want to get laid." It is a triumph of the women, then, that they are able to hold out, while the men capitulate, doubled over with painful erections. The play celebrates the phallic powers of peace, in all its wide-ranging, life-generating, and life-enjoying senses.

In *The Acharnians*, Aristophanes' first surviving play, the old farmer Dikaiopolis performs phallic rites for Dionysus to celebrate his separate truce with the Spartans:

> *Grant, O Lord, your blessings now on me,*
> *Freed from the army's service and returned to yours.*
> *And let this Peace of Thirty Years endure,*
> *And bring us health, wealth, and true happiness.*

The religious ceremony concludes with a hymn to Phales, the personified phallus. Dikaiopolis grows in wealth and personal influence as the forces of war and militarism (represented by Lamachos) are exposed in their exemplary adversity. The play ends with the drunken Dikaiopolis, supported on each arm by a beautiful whore, reeling off stage with a huge, full wineskin, the prize he has just been awarded in the drinking contest. In *Peace*, Aristophanes' most overtly festive comedy, the farmer Trygaeus crowns his crazy expedition to Zeus on a dung-beetle by rescuing Peace, Opora (i.e., Harvest), and Theoria (i.e., Holiday) and bringing them back to earth. Theoria is undressed and presented nude to the Athenian Senate, while Trygaeus marries Opora in a triumphant party in honor of Hymen, the god of marriage. Gods and mortals are freely mixed, and the play celebrates themes of much wider scope than the finding or reconciliation of the lovers so common in New Comedy.

Rabelais is undoubtedly the most "aristophanic" of Aristophanes' successors, as Bakhtin has so ably demonstrated. Of English authors, perhaps only Skelton and Chaucer are close to Aristophanes in spirit. Shakespeare has sometimes been claimed as a kindred soul, but his festive comedy is much less broad than that of Aristophanes. Falstaff is fat and gross, but a witty, eloquent, histrionic speaker, who celebrates the virtues of youth against all serious contenders. Falstaff is the wily man, the ironic impostor, who knows how to have the best of all arguments. Although he indulges in the fructifying and refreshing powers of strong drink and fornication, his revelry lacks some of the spontaneous and naive quality of Aristophanes' heroes. Falstaff is perhaps too sophisticated and self-conscious to qualify for aristophanic comedy. He is not the "little man," who suddenly carries us with him into explosive and triumphant celebration. There is plenty of celebration in Falstaff, but it lacks the ritual underpinnings of Aristophanes.

Ben Jonson is more convincingly aristophanic in spirit than Shakespeare, and his plays demonstrate a more compelling achievement in the genre of festive comedy. Jonson himself was a burly man, given to bursts of violent anger—he killed a fellow actor, Gabriel Spencer, in a duel—and seemingly a person of more wildly contrasted moods of depression and elation than the more even-tempered Shakespeare. Shakespeare never tries for the intense and bursting fullness of Jonson's comedy at its best, nor for the manic and almost hysterical frenzy of Jonson's climaxes—hyperbolical and overdone perhaps, but still very energetic and moving.

Consider the grand scope of *Bartholomew Fair* (1614). If the fair is a microcosm of English society, then it is not only a representative community, but also one that is copious, overfull, bursting with abundant life and vitality. What an extraordinary set of characters we have in this play. First, there is the Littlewit circle, consisting of John Littlewit, a proctor (or business agent), amateur of choice language and literature, and writer of a classically derived puppet play; his servant Solomon; his wife, Win Littlewit; her mother, Dame Purecraft, a Puritan widow of force and cunning; Zeal-of-the-land Busy, her suitor and a forked-tongue Puritan hypocrite of the hyperbolical vein; Winwife, his rival for Dame Purecraft, and a gentleman; Quarlous, the companion of Winwife, and a gamester. Second, visiting the fair are the following: Bartholomew Cokes, a foolish but good-hearted and rich young gentleman, and Humphrey Wasp, his testy manservant and keeper; Adam Overdo, a justice of the peace, disguised as mad Arthur of Bradley to hunt out enormities in the fair; his wife, Dame Overdo, who is also sister of Cokes; Grace Wellborn, his ward; and Trouble-all, a madman, demanding of one and all if they have Justice Overdo's warrant for what they are doing. Third, we have the proprietors of the fair: Lantern Leatherhead, a seller of hobbyhorses (a child's toy) and puppeteer; Joan Trash, a gingerbread-woman; Ezekiel Edgworth, a refined cutpurse, who works in tandem with Nightingale, a ballad-singer; Ursula, the fat pig-woman, who sells roast pig and strong drink and is also a bit of a bawd; Mooncalf, her tapster. Lastly, among miscellaneous and disorderly persons are the following: Jordan Knockem, a furious horse-courser (or horse-trader) and part-time pimp; Val Cutting, a roarer (or bully); Captain Whit, a bawd; Punk Alice, a mistress of the game (or prostitute); three watchmen named Haggis, Bristle, and Poacher, a beadle; Costermonger or fruit seller; Northern, a clothier; Puppy, a wrestler; Filcher and Sharkwell, two doorkeepers at the puppet play; assorted passersby; a corncutter; a tinderbox-man (presumably someone who sells mousetraps); and puppets in *The Ancient Modern History of Hero and Leander, Otherwise Called The Touchstone of True Love.*

Bartholomew Fair is bursting with characters and a variety of in-

cidents and action. It is a rich, copious play that celebrates, at a
very basic level, the sheer fun and vitality of life. Persons of good
natural impulse triumph over their more sophisticated, more cunning, and more self-interested rivals. Thus, the generosity and good-
heartedness of the foolish boy, Bartholomew Cokes—who is a
"cokes," or simpleton and ninny—confute the tightness and nasti-
ness of his angry keeper, Humphrey Wasp. The lovableness of
Cokes is all that is needed for him to succeed at Batholomew Fair,
where he endears himself to everyone by buying up all the toys,
gauds, and trash offered to him. As Wasp puts it, with uncharac-
teristic lyric grace:

> Would the Fair and all the drums and rattles in't were
> i' your belly for me! They are already i' your brain; he that
> had the means to travel your head, now, should meet finer
> sights than any are i' the Fair, and make a finer voyage
> on't, to see it all hung with cockle-shells, pebbles, fine
> wheat-straws, and here and there a chicken's feather and a
> cobweb. (1.5.86–91)

The heroes of the fair are the mad people, those who are wild,
unrestrained, and unlicensed in speech and in imagination, while
the villains are cold, calculating, and hypocritical. But there really
are no villains at all, since even the Puritans (whom Jonson de-
tested) have an extravagance of expression and style that is attractive. Everything turns on hyperbole. The greatest living hyperbole
is Ursula, the pig-woman, who sweats profusely as she roasts her
pigs: "I am all fire and fat, Nightingale; I shall e'en melt away to
the first woman, a rib again, I am afraid. I do water the ground in
knots as I go, like a great garden-pot; you may follow me by the S's
I make." This sounds like Falstaff, but a larger and more lubricious
character, and one not so self-conscious of the effects he is produc-
ing.

Jonson's characters are conceived on the "humors" plan, in
which one dominant preoccupation or character trait (the "master
passion") motivates their speech and behavior. This singleness of
purpose concentrates their energies; they are always fully wound
up and they are propelled forward by a furious certainty about

their own destiny. They are all zealots of one kind or another—and here Jonson borrowed from Puritan "zeal"—even Justice Overdo, who disguises himself as mad Arthur of Bradley in order to personally discover the hidden crimes of the fair. He pursues his aim with an ardor and a frenzy that go beyond any mere desire for justice:

> Now to my enormities: look upon me, o London! and see
> me, o Smithfield [the site of the fair]! the example of
> justice and mirror of magistrates, the true top of formality
> and scourge of enormity. Hearken unto my labors and but
> observe my discoveries, and compare Hercules with me, if
> thou dar'st, of old; or Columbus, Magellan, or our
> countryman Drake of later times. Stand forth you weeds
> of enormity, and spread. (5.6.33–39)

He is finally, of course, put out of his humor and forced to acknowledge that he is "but Adam, flesh and blood," but while active he is a grand, misguided, comic overreacher.

In *The Alchemist* (1610), Jonson also deals in illusions. Subtle, the alchemist, is a wonder-worker and magician, and the scope of his activity extends far beyond alchemy. His dupes are not dupes at all, because Subtle gives good value for the money he receives: he tickles the imagination of all his clients and makes them heroic, almost mythological figures in their own eyes. The transformations in Genet's *Balcony* resemble those in *The Alchemist*, as ordinary mortals assume new and commanding roles. This indulgence of the imagination and glorious, gratified wish fulfillment lends itself to the feeling of festive comedy. We are under the impression that the characters are at play rather than at work, and despite a bit of moralizing here and there, *The Alchemist* is not very purposive or instructive. At the end the alchemical apparatus explodes, Lovewit returns to claim his house, and Subtle and Doll escape over the wall, but we feel that the demonstration has changed nothing and that Subtle and Doll—and Face, too—will set up shop again in another locale. The anarchic comic energies have not been destroyed, but only temporarily regulated and contained.

Sir Epicure Mammon is the great imaginer in this play, and it is at his bidding and expense that the alchemical operations are going forward. Sir Epicure suffers from satyriasis of the imagination. His orgasmic vision of luxury, once the philosopher's stone has been discovered, echoes Jonson's classical sources:

> *I will have all my beds blown up, not stuffed:*
> *Down is too hard. And then mine oval room*
> *Filled with such pictures as Tiberius took*
> *From Elephantis, and dull Aretine*
> *But coldly imitated. Then, my glasses [mirrors]*
> *Cut in more subtle angles, to disperse*
> *And multiply the figures as I walk*
> *Naked between my succubae [enticing female spirits]. My*
>   *mists*
> *I'll have of perfume, vapored 'bout the room,*
> *To loose our selves in; and my baths like pits*
> *To fall into; from whence we will come forth*
> *And roll us dry in gossamer and roses. (2.2.41–52)*

Mammon's sensual paradise contains within it hints of his own limited and tawdry imagination; it suggests Fellini's *Satyricon* rather than Milton's *Paradise Lost*, especially in its vision of sunken bathtubs, air mattresses, perfumed humidifiers, dirty pictures, and a plethora of cut-glass mirrors. Mammon's bad taste endows his poetic utopia with a certain charming tackiness: the character, with his unfortunate "itch of mind," is definitely life-size (or smaller).

Similarly, the little lawyer's clerk, Dapper, is inflamed by his soon-to-be-consummated meeting with the Fairy Queen (as played by Doll Common, the strumpet), while he awaits her, gagged with ginger-bread, in a privy—"Fortune's privy lodgings," as Subtle explains it. After all of the knightly trials he has been put through, when Dapper finally encounters "his gracious aunt," he is so awestruck he can only say: "I cannot speak for joy." Festive comedy seems to be celebrating the fact that even Dapper can have his apocalyptic vision and be incarnated as a known minion of the Fairy Queen. That he is mercilessly tricked, extorted, and bamboozled only gives added poignancy to the power and resilience of the comic imagination.

V

Comedy in Theory and in Practice: Seven Aspects of the Comic Hero

In a moment of anxious banter, the conundrum-making Fool tells Lear: "The reason why the seven stars are no moe [more] than seven is a pretty reason." Lear sees the point at once: "Because they are not eight," and the Fool applauds his wit: "Yes indeed. Thou wouldst make a good Fool" (1.5.35–39). The reason why there are only seven aspects of the comic hero is much the same as the Fool's seven stars. The following speculations are offered in a playful spirit. From the extensive literature, I have selected seven proposi-

143

tions that may serve as a groundwork for understanding the theory of comedy and as a sampling of the wider historical discussion.

The theory of comedy is a subject that is neither entertaining nor comic in itself. It is surprising how little formal philosophy has contributed to our understanding of comedy, especially the kind that makes you laugh. Despite the tradition of Democritus, the Laughing Philosopher celebrated in Robert Burton's *Anatomy of Melancholy* (1621), laughter has always embarrassed philosophers, whereas psychologists and physiologists are at least stimulated to measure it and to understand its context and its causes. Is man uniquely gelastic, the only animal that laughs? If that is true, then we need not be ashamed of an act that shows us to be a little lower than the angels and separates us from the entire animal creation. If it turns out that animals have their own kind of laughter, still, no one has yet suggested that plants laugh, regardless of how respon- sive they may be to music and affectionate conversation.

I postulate a hypothetical comic hero with at least seven charac- teristics in order to explore some basic assumptions about the art of comedy. The comic hero is certainly not limited to these seven points, and readers will want to supply their own list of proposi- tions. Also, no comic hero could possibly be aware of these charac- teristics, because that would destroy the comic effect, which de- pends for its force on sincerity, simplicity, naivety, and unlimited self-indulgence. The seven traits are not, of course, fully consistent with each other and may actually be contradictory. Thus, if the comic hero is invulnerable and omnipotent, how can he also be a realist who affirms the life force? Or if he indulges in wish fulfill- ment and fantasy gratification and play without any ulterior pur- pose, why should he also suffer from comic paranoia, as if laughter were an essential defense against a hostile reality?

The art of comedy is so broad in its scope that it includes contra- dictions at opposite ends of the gamut, but, more importantly, comedy deals in illusions. The comic hero may imagine himself to be invulnerable and omnipotent, but this is usually pure fantasy, since he is typically the little man trying to manipulate a recalci- trant and hostile reality. Dream materials play a large role in com- edy, and we must distinguish between what is imagined and what is more or less true. One is usually played off against the other. Besides, the comic hero is also a trickster and ritual clown, hopelessly evasive, and difficult to measure against objective criteria. All these characteristics tend to separate the comic hero very sharply from the more realistic and more moral assumptions of tragedy. The comic hero usually displays an anarchic, chaotic energy that cannot be contained or fulfilled within the boundaries of plot. The resolution of the dramatic action in comedy is generally not so purposive or so pointed as it is in tragedy, which seems to realize preordained ends. Comedy is not normative or teleological as tragedy generally is and therefore doesn't lend itself to the demonstration of ethical points.

The comic hero imagines himself to be invulnerable and omnipotent.

The comic hero is a dreamlike figure who seems oblivious to human limitations. He can easily walk in the air—as in Ionesco's play, *The Aerial Pedestrians*, or *A Stroll in the Air* (*Les Piétons de l'Air*)—hover, glide, and perform remarkable aerodynamic feats without any effort at all. The weightless, balletic grace is essential to the comic effect, because any hint of exertion—any sweat—pricks the bubble of illusion and makes the comic hero mortal like us. Mortality is an assumption of tragedy, where the identification with the hero generates the sympathy that is indispensable for tragic effect.

In the Harold Lloyd movie, *Safety Last*, we see him dangling raffishly from the hour-hand of a clock far above the street, which beckons menacingly like the abyss below, but Harold Lloyd manages to maintain an energetic, altogether business-like expression (see Figure 11). He isn't scared, and the terror we feel has definite limits, since we have ruled out the possibility that he might fall. He is invulnerable, omnipotent—maybe just lucky—and we follow his high-altitude act with the comic exhilaration of danger that will surely be overcome. Of course, it is only a film, it is not actually happening at this very moment, and the dangers have been safely neutralized by the medium: God's in his heaven and the film is in the can.

One might speculate in what sense a daring and death-defying act is comic. There is, of course, an element of fearful expectation on the part of the spectators that is different from watching a movie. Will the high-wire equilibrist lose his balance, or the acrobat flying through the air fail to make contact with his waiting partner? Will Elvin Bale, the star of the Ringling Brothers' circus, manage to keep his balance while walking blindfolded on the giant, gyrating gyro-wheel? Does the presence of a safety net make the experience *more* or *less* comic? And why do some highly-gifted professionals refuse to perform with a net? Isn't the sense of danger essential to the effect? The beauty of the performance depends on our inner certainty that, by some special magic, the performer is invulnerable. Through a long and arduous training, he has learned how to free himself from the troublesome demands of gravity. His perfect harmony and balance make him different from the spectators. He is not supposed to fall, because then the illusion would be broken and he would be like us. This godlike quality of acrobats, aerialists, and stunt men shows their mastery of human limitations and endows them with enormous romantic appeal. Another way of looking at it is to see the circus performance as the triumph of difficulty overcome, the perfectly gratuitous act that proves man's immortality.

Buster Keaton was our great example of a comic innocent who could not be harmed by experience. Since he was also a trained acrobat and equilibrist, he had a knack for making the most impossible feats—such as switching motorcycles at full speed or hanging on at the edge of a waterfall—seem disarmingly simple and innocuous. In *The Love Nest*, Keaton stands on a ladder *perpendicular* to the ship, calmly surveying the nautical scene through what appear to be opera glasses. He is wonderfully at ease in this extraordinary position (see Figure 12). The great chases, with or without Keystone Cops or their equivalent, were always meant to demonstrate the invulnerability and omnipotence of the comic hero, who could never conceivably be overcome by the material forces he scorned. The very magnitude of the opposition proves the futility of mere

Figure 11. The Comic Hero on the Edge of Disaster: Harold Lloyd in *Safety Last* (Pathé, 1923); *The Museum of Modern Art/Film Stills Archive.*

physical prowess. Lightness, agility, dexterity, the cunning of intelligence, the subtlety of spirit, the ingenuity and resourcefulness of wit—these are the qualities that ultimately triumph. Mere numbers, even of frenzied savages as in *The Navigator,* mean nothing at all. Despite any temporary setbacks, which only stimulate the comic hero to newer and more daring exertions, we are always aware that nothing can ultimately stop him.

In *The General,* Keaton's delivery of a train through Confederate lines is literally a heroic feat, but, unlike authentic melodrama, the dangers are unreal—they are merely meant to spur the hero on. Instead of suspense, we experience comic euphoria, which rises to a grand and triumphant climax that only mimics the climax and dé-nouement of melodrama. We are made to feel that the comic hero can do no wrong (just as the melodramatic villain can do no right), and even Keaton's seeming missteps and accidents and moments of forgetfulness have unforeseen fortunate results. In Figure 13 from *The General*, we see him, with wonderful aplomb, listening in on a cannon that is about to explode—and doesn't. Perhaps flaws are in-troduced in order to tease our conviction that the comic hero is in-vulnerable and omnipotent, just as the high-wire performer often pretends to slip or stumble in order to inject a feeling of danger into his act. Or there is the classic turn of the drunk, who absent-mindedly strays out onto the high-wire and wanders about without letting on that he knows where he is. He only becomes frightened when he realizes, in the middle of his act, what is happening; before that he is totally oblivious to danger. With Buster Keaton and other innocent and nonchalant daredevils, we have the distinct impression that they are favored by the gods and therefore could not blunder even if they wanted to.

To make a crosscultural and interdisciplinary comparison, Shake-speare's Falstaff may have much in common with Buster Keaton. Both are totally impervious to the blows of Fortune, not from any stoic fortitude, but merely because both function outside the sys-tem of physical constraints, including the law of gravity (in Fal-staff's world, "gravity," meaning sobriety and uprightness, can be misheard as "gravy," as in *Henry IV, Part 2* 1.2.166–68). Both have achieved a kind of weightlessness—if such a paradox can be sus-tained for a fat man so gross as Falstaff. He may be fat but he is never shown to be ungraceful, and his weightlessness is only a way of indicating his ultimate freedom from the very body with which he is burdened and of which he is so inordinately proud. It must be clear by now that the question posed by Maurice Morgann, the eighteenth-century critic, whether Falstaff is really a coward is en-tirely irrelevant, since he is so clearly protected from the dangers of military encounter. Like matter, a Falstaff can neither be created nor destroyed: he exists in a timeless continuum. His undisputed status as the comic hero protects him against sword thrusts, bul-

Figure 12. The Comic Hero as Acrobat: Buster Keaton in *The Love Nest* (First National, 1923; often mistakenly attributed to *The Navigator*, 1924); *The Museum of Modern Art/Film Stills Archive.*

Figure 13. The Comic Hero in Tune with the World of Things: Buster Keaton in *The General* (United Artists, 1927); *The Museum of Modern Art/Film Stills Archive.*

lets, and other hostile and destructive acts. He is literally invulnerable.

Shakespeare mixes Falstaff into the military scenes in order to juxtapose two different kinds of reality. The noble antagonists on the field of battle are all very vulnerable, partly because their sense of honor demands that they kill or be killed. Falstaff has no intention of doing either. His surprising capture of the French prisoner Coleville and his pretended victory over the dead Hotspur are pure parody of the heroic activity taking place all around him—parody and satiric commentary on the grisly values of war—and this may be one way of introducing a counter-theme to the heroics of battle.

Falstaff doesn't like the "grinning honor" of the dead Sir Walter Blunt, and he calls in question the high-flown honor, much celebrated by Hotspur, that can only lead to death. In this sense, the comic hero is not only invulnerable and omnipotent, but he is also a scorner of death and the power death has to tempt men into its clutches.

The comic hero indulges in wish fulfillment and fantasy gratification.

Wish fulfillment and fantasy gratification sound like serious charges to bring against our defenseless, but luckily hypothetical, comic hero. Freud is constantly berating jokesters and laughers for their infantile and regressive impulses, as if, by committing themselves to jokes, they were refusing the rigors of adult life. It's true that the joke-teller demands instant gratification. It won't do to tell him that you will think about his joke and let him know if you find it funny, as in the old saying: "Tell an Englishman jokes when he's young so he will have something to laugh about when he's old."

Physiologists have connected laughter with two other involuntary activities: orgasm and epileptic seizure. All three are muscle spasms, which reach a climax and then subside. The intense climax satisfies the original impulse and purges it, so that one may well say, to twist the adage: after laughter the soul is sad. Weeping is apparently not the organic opposite of laughter or really analogous to it at all. For one thing, it is inspirational (drawing in the breath) rather than expirational and explosive as laughter is. In laughing, we are trying to get rid of some overwhelming and irresistible stimulus. Our response to tickling, which is the most fully studied aspect of this subject, may be protective and defensive: we attempt to withdraw the threatened part from the line of attack (or potential attack). This is like the child's threat: "I bet I can make you laugh," as if the involuntary laughter were a sign of weakness and capitulation. Freud connects laughter, like sex, with the suppressed, repressed, and unconscious activities of the Id, and his book on jokes is an offshoot of his monumental study of dreams. His analysis of joke-material (the inimitable *Witzwerk*) proceeds along the same lines as his analysis of dreams (the *Traumwerk*) and slips of the tongue, with the seemingly random manifest content expressing specific latent meanings.

Some alert intellect, taking Freud's brilliant theories as a basis, could produce a better book on wit and laughter than Freud did. *Jokes and Their Relation to the Unconscious* (1905) doesn't do justice to the liveliness of its writer's imagination. Aside from its collection of ancient Jewish jokes—"Have you taken a bath?" "Why, is there one missing?" or "I take a bath regularly once a month whether I need it or not"—Freud's book is ponderous and theoretical. It sets the reader wondering whether Freud was deprived of a sense of humor. The book labors the obvious in its analysis of jokes, and it tries to make nebulous distinctions between different kinds of comedy. Yet, next to Bergson's essay on laughter in 1900, it is the best book we have on the subject. It makes the essential and unforgettable link between laughter and the irrational, the unconscious, and the instinctive drives of man. There is a natural and necessary impulse to laugh that demands expression, and we need laughter in order to function as human beings.

The basic mechanism of dreams and of comedy is wish fulfillment. The comic hero imagines himself as not only adequate for every situation that may present itself, but infinitely superior to all other men. He is never at a loss for an answer, and this must be central to our understanding of comic superiority. Not only an answer, but a beautiful, witty, eloquent answer. Wish fulfillment implies unlimited versatility and intelligence. The clown's quick rejoinders use the traditional logical forms of *tu quoque* ("the same to you") and *quid pro quo* ("tit for tat"), which are the hallmarks of comic resourcefulness: any answer can itself be answered, the comedian can return and improve on someone else's witty comment, he must always have the last word, and, most importantly, he can never be put down or embarrassed. In our complex social life, this in itself is a form of omnipotence and invulnerability.

The Clown-gravedigger in Act V of *Hamlet*, for example, is a masterful equivocator, who delights in deflecting every one of Hamlet's well-meant questions and conversational gibes. Hamlet is no match for the gravedigger's logic-chopping and punning wit,

Figure 14. Man versus the Machine: Charlie Chaplin and Chester Conklin in *Modern Times* (United Artists, 1936); *The Museum of Modern Art /Film Stills Archive.*

and Hamlet breaks off the conversation with the distinct feeling of having been had. Comic heroes are usually great talkers: Falstaff and W. C. Fields, Plautus's Pseudolus and Groucho Marx, Oscar Wilde's Ernest and just about any of the ferociously relaxed characters of Shaw, who all resemble their creator. In the silent movies, a gestural language replaced words, but the triumphs of Keaton, Chaplin, and even Ben Turpin were comparable in form to those of spoken dialogue. All expressed a wish-fulfillment superiority to ordinary, plodding, embarrassed mortals.

Chaplin was the thin-man type—small, wiry, delicate, sad, but infinitely graceful and agile. As the tramp, he cultivated the illusion of being an outcast from society, an image of failure and rejection. This gave a special ironic edge to his heroic visions in *The Great Dictator*, or his grappling single-handedly with industrial machinery in *Modern Times*. There are some beautifully lyric sequences in that film, as in Figure 14, where Chaplin plays his oilcan as if it were a recorder and dances forward on the gears to Chester Conklin's astonishment and disbelief. Since language is excluded in the silent movie, Chaplin's witty rejoinders to bullies and oppressors are always physical: an expression of contempt or disgust, a quick step or motion by which the antagonist is accidentally knocked down, the use of some random object that happens to be at hand to express an animate meaning.

The silent-movie technique was so highly developed and so sophisticated in its use of sight gags and visual meanings that the introduction of sound produced an immediate anticlimax. Chaplin made marvelous use of dream sequences, in which fantasy and reality are deliberately blurred, as in the shoe-eating episode of *The Gold Rush*. This kind of presentation translates wish fulfillment and fantasy gratification into the literal images we see before us on the screen. An early classic of this kind is the short film by Edwin S. Porter, *Dream of a Rarebit Fiend* (1906), in which the melted cheese of the Welsh rarebit produces nocturnal visions of an Arabian Night's journey by bed (see Figure 15). This film ventures into the no-man's land of comic nightmare, in which the dreamer is able to effect an ingenious triumph over his fears.

The links between comedy and dreams are very specific, especially in the mechanism of free association, by which the dreamer and the comic hero jump from point to point by intuitive leaps and without any necessary, logical connection. There is, of course, a dream logic, as Freud so painstakingly demonstrated, different from the commonsense logic of ordinary waking experience. Dream logic is symbolically self-contained and self-consistent, and the leaps are all generated by a train of thought which expresses important preoccupations. The dream world of the *Wizard of Oz* is a projection of the cozy farm scenes with which the film begins, and Shakespeare's *Midsummer Night's Dream* uses the dream sequences in the wood to play out conflicts in the real world of Athens.

Dream technique allows for a fluidity of movement that is not possible in everyday life. Displacement of real to imagined experience, distortion of visual images, substitution of dream logic for rational sequence and causality, endless repetition and variations of fixed patterns can all be freely used to emphasize a certain mood or turn of thought. Suddenly, everything is possible, and from this unlimited freedom come the startling puns and new associations out of which comedy is created. It is important to insist that the making of comedy is an imaginative activity that seeks to recombine and refashion the raw materials of experience into something different, something created by the mind, something essentially metaphorical. These high claims for the powers of comedy indicate that it is not a "realistic" art at all. It may draw on the humble materials of daily life that tragedy in the high style rejects, but this is only the beginning. The comic imagination uses these materials for its own purposes. As in dreams, the facts are thoroughly transformed by distortion, overemphasis, imaginary dialogue, wordplay, incongruity, and other personalizing devices, so that the imagined reality has little resemblance to the reality with which we began. To put it simply, the objective reality is fundamentally changed by the churning and turbulent processes of wish fulfillment and fantasy gratification.

The comic hero engages in play without any ulterior purpose.

Huizinga, the Dutch historian and author of *The Waning of the Middle Ages*, reminds us forcefully that man is an animal who needs to play, that play is an instinctual impulse that must be satisfied. Man is *Homo ludens* (which is the title of Huizinga's fascinating book on play), and to ignore this is to obscure an essential characteristic of all living creatures. Phylogenetically speaking, how far back would Huizinga be willing to go? Do amoeba play, and are water spiders really skipping and frolicking on the surface of a pond? To what extent do we anthropomorphize and animate the nonhuman creation? We might as well ask if dogs really laugh,

Figure 15. Comic Nightmare: Flying over the Brooklyn Bridge (Edwin S. Porter's *Dream of a Rarebit Fiend*, 1906); *The Museum of Modern Art / Film Stills Archive.*

even though they can almost exactly mimic human laughter. But play is something more fundamental than laughter, and it satisfies imperative physiological needs. The insistent babbling of small children—sometimes pure nonsense phrases—fulfills a need for expression that cannot be resisted. Or mere high spirits, if there is such a thing, may find an outlet in a purely physical activity like running. There is a sense in which running, or skipping, or even singing in the shower, are completely joyous activities without any ulterior motive. Huizinga's argument depends strongly on animal physiology, where play is a powerful physical drive. Once the theory is applied to human beings, however, complications arise.

The basic issue is whether play is purposive. Is it an activity performed solely for its own sake, a need that seeks its own satisfaction apart from other needs, or does it work together with other needs and does it express, either directly or symbolically, the general preoccupations of the player at any particular moment? It's difficult to see how play can be isolated from all other human expressions, even though it may have its own motives and dynamics. We seem to be involved in a fundamental quibble on the word "play." We not only play, but we also play at: we not only engage in motor activities, but we also act out roles; we play parts as well as games, and the histrionic meaning of "play" is unavoidable. Children not only play ball, but they also play house and play doctor, and it is not possible to separate these activities.

Play is a form of impersonation. It may well be that acting is as basic a human need as mere physical play, or, more properly, acting may be deeply involved in all games. We play at baseball, and, specifically, we play catcher, pitcher, first baseman, etc. A different stance and even a different set of abilities are involved in each of these positions. To runners, for example, there is a world of difference between long and short distances—not just physically, but also psychologically, and long-distance running, with its proverbial loneliness, attracts a different temperament from sprinting. The games we play are a distinct expression of our personality. We don't just play in general, but we restrict our play to games that are suitable for us. In this way, physical and histrionic senses of "play" begin to merge.

Freud, and Freudian critics, tend to stigmatize play as infantile regression, and their theories of comedy are so highly purposive that mere play seems to drop out entirely. But this simplifies and rationalizes motives. If comedy is a way of mastering a fearful, uncertain, and mysterious reality, we may play at roles and positions for some temporary advantages and without being fully committed to them. Freud so thoroughly excludes children from his account of comedy that he fails to see how we may be continuing childlike attitudes and responses in our humor. Even if we admit that aggression is a powerful component in many jokes, we still need to define the exact status of that aggression. We may be playing at the ag-

gressor with a histrionic audacity that may frighten even us, as
Charlie Chaplin seemed to scare himself as the Great Dictator. The
status of this aggression is ambiguous. It's like a group of children
telling ghost stories during a blackout who wind up being terrified.
The play element is the part that is difficult to account for. We are
kidding around and we are serious at one and the same time, and
the exact proportions of each may baffle us. We may not really dis-
cern the strength of our own motives until we test the reactions of
others. They may either inspire us to go on or dampen our enthusiasm.

The Freudian account of dirty jokes is also unsatisfactory, because Freud minimizes so ungenerously the element of play. Sexual
activity may belong much more securely to the domain of play
than Freud would admit. Freud seemed to think that the mere exposure of the genitals (or talk about it) would stimulate ordinary
persons into frenzied grabbing and groping. Unfortunately, sexual
motivations are not so simple, and dirty jokes provide gratifications
that may not be directly related to sexual activity at all. In these
jokes there is a definite need for outrage, as determined by what
the Supreme Court calls "community standards" at any particular
time or place, and a definite need for wit, but whether the telling of
dirty jokes is intended as a form of seduction is doubtful. At a
party, the tellers of dirty jokes are engaged in their own, appropri-
ately hedonistic activity, while the seducers and ravishers are otherwise occupied in other rooms of the house. Joke-telling is play in
its own right—and play on the dangerous edges of propriety—but
hardly a substitute for rape. As the evening wears on, the dirty
jokes tend to get bolder and more daring, as if the tellers were
challenging each other to outdo some ultimate taboo, but the struggle is clearly a battle of wits rather than one of sexual energies,
however repressed and sublimated.

It is interesting to observe how faithfully dirty jokes follow conventions. The sexual permissiveness of our society has not destroyed dirty jokes, as one might have predicted, but has consider-
ably raised the standards. It is not enough merely to use dirty
words and to name the forbidden parts, since raw sex doesn't have
the shock effect that it used to. A certain sophistication is needed,
as in the *Private Eye* cartoon (see Figure 16), which shows a series

Figure 16. An Old Joke in a New Context (*Private Eye*,
November 12, 1965; *reprinted by permission*).

of photographs of typically bored, upper-class persons of more
than middle age, with the following comic-strip dialogue: (1) Man:
"Apparently there was this man in bed with this woman . . ." (2)
"and the man said: 'Do you smoke after intercourse?' " (3) "and *she*
said: 'I don't know. I've never looked.' " (4) Different Man: "Go
on! What happened next?" Woman: "Good evening!" The final
frame is meant to mock the proverbial inability of the English to
understand jokes. This is an old joke in new guise, but it demands

a certain mental agility to get the point. It is not the sexual subject in itself that arouses laughter, but the satirical, mocking tone.

In his analyses of literary material, Freud persistently errs by confusing the subject matter with the real purpose. Even though he insists on the distinction between manifest and latent content, he doesn't make proper allowances for an aesthetic and a play dimension apart from purely personal, psychological needs. Nor does Freud take adequate account of pleasure, in its idiosyncratic and variable forms. There is a directness in play that Freud tends to ignore, preferring the more sophisticated proposition that everything is likely to be displaced and symbolic and to mean something else. But play is creative and aesthetic and needs no ulterior explanation or justification. The pleasure we take in play is associated with a childlike absorption and intensity, which is nonobjective, nonpurposive, and certainly not to be disdained, especially by adults.

The comic hero is a realist who celebrates the body and affirms the life force.

Paradoxically, comedy can, at different moments, rejoice in the triumph over the material limitations of the body and also indulge in the equally powerful impulse to enjoy the pleasures of the body. No theoretician of comedy has ever claimed that eating, drinking, sleeping, fornicating, or any other pleasure of the senses was comic in and for itself. Even in the lowest kinds of farce or pantomime, the humor of the senses is derived either from hyperbole or understatement—a skillful exaggeration of what the audience might expect, or a teasing frustration of the expectations that have been aroused. One can imagine the methodical consumption of several hundred pancakes (on the lines of the joke in which the analyst reassures his patient: "There's nothing wrong with liking pancakes. I have a closet [or steamer trunk] full of them myself"). Or we can picture a striptease photographed in reverse (either in slow or in speeded-up motion), but eating or sex in themselves have no inherent comic force. The point is that the comic hero, by his very nature, needs to declare himself the patron of everything real, physical, material, enjoyable, and the enemy of all abstractions, moral principles, seriousness, and joylessness. This is a matter of basic allegiance to the life force.

According to literary tradition, fat people are funny. This is either supported or not supported by real life, depending on the sensitivity of fat people to cultural stereotypes. Weight Watchers, of course, understands the tradition so well that it can effectively undermine it from within. Rabelais' Gargantua and Pantagruel, Chaucer's Wife of Bath, Skelton's Elynour Rummyng, Shakespeare's Falstaff, Jonson's Ursula the pig-woman are just a few characters who come immediately to mind—all of whom celebrate the richness, copiousness, zest, and infinite variety of life. They are large persons both literally and metaphorically, and their expansiveness and verbal exuberance are directly related to their physique. They eat, drink, and fornicate with the same energetic abandon with which they speak. All the juices flow together, but our interest is in their comic imagination rather than in their stomach and private parts. Food, drink, and sex fuel their wit, which cannot operate as a purely intellectual faculty.

In his influential theory of comedy, Henri Bergson separates those who celebrate the life force (and are therefore the makers of comedy) from those who impose a mechanical rigidity on the free flow of experience (and thereby qualify as the butts of comedy). The comic hero is typically someone who believes in daily life and its round of assorted and unanticipated pleasures, who is optimistic about the future, and who, unlike the tragic hero, has little or no interest in the past. He is a hedonist who lives for the moment, and wit becomes a lifestyle that replaces any moral, ethical, or religious commitments. The fat man, if he is fat enough, is himself a hyperbole in the flesh, an impressive "too much," a living exaggeration, a creative overreacher and overdoer. This is the source of his comic strength.

Another aspect of the fat man is that he is, in the best sense of the word, a grotesque. He violates the norm at every point, and his very existence titillates our fancy. Like all grotesques, he is literally incredible. Starting from here, we can discover qualities that may be played off against the grossness of his physical being. The late and much-lamented Zero Mostel, for example, danced with ex-

traordinary delicacy, and the fineness of his sensibility was emphasized to good effect in *A Funny Thing Happened on the Way to the
Forum* (based on Plautus—see Figure 17), *Rhinoceros*, Mel Brooks's
The Producers, and the recent Woody Allen movie, *The Front*. To
everyone's surprise and delight, within that oafish and clumsy
body of Zero Mostel dwelt the soul of a poet—trapped, as it were,

Figure 17. Comic Grace: Zero Mostel Dancing in *A Funny Thing
Happened on the Way to the Forum* (United Artists, 1966); *Movie Star
News.*

and struggling to emerge. Wit is always the opposite of grossness, so that the comic fat man always enjoys the advantages of the dualistic paradox of soul versus body. The keenness of Falstaff's intelligence, the acuity of his wit, the alertness of his replies, the sharpness of his verbal attack all belie the fatness of his body. It is as if the fat man's body were a disguise he adopted to conceal his trenchant qualities. And again we are back at the persistent dualism of the fine spirit forced to inhabit an inappropriate body. But without this grotesque dualism the immediate comic response would be lost.

Extremely thin, wiry persons, with infinitely sad faces, can achieve grotesque effects comparable to fat men, but they are a much rarer breed. Perhaps Don Quixote fits here, as set against his plump servant, Sancho Panza, or the brilliant comedy team of Laurel and Hardy, who have a symbiotic relationship to each other. In many of W. C. Fields's films there is a sharp-featured, hollow-cheeked man (played by Bill Wolf), who perfectly fits the thin-man stereotype. He says nothing, but stares vacantly into space in a mute, poker-faced indictment of reality. He is gaunt, almost deathly in pallor, and the fact that he never laughs—or that he is totally incapable of laughter—is the source of almost uncontrollable mirth in the audience. In Figure 18 from *Follow the Boys*, we see Bill Wolf in a grotesquely ill-fitting zoot suit, being handled by the cigar-smoking, pool-shooting Fields as if he were an inanimate object. He was the perfect straightman for Fields, who worked this unworkable zombie with increasingly predictable futility. The thin man's role is complicated by his inability to make, in his person, the kind of physical affirmation the fat man does. The thin man can deliver a powerful shock to our comfortable assumptions; we try to sympathize with his physical dearth, but he rejects our commiseration with mute superiority. He is proud of his negative distinction.

The intense awareness of the body that the fat man forces on us (and the thin man, too, by default, if he is only thin enough to merit our attention) is one of the richest sources of jokes and comic situations. There is a good deal of anxiety that energizes our nervous laughter here. Sid Caesar had a beautiful skit in *Ten from Your Show of Shows*, in which, at a formal piano recital, all of his custom-

Figure 18. W. C. Fields and the Cadaverous Bill Wolf in *Follow the Boys* (Universal, 1944); Movie Star News.

ary body noises were wildly amplified. His neck when he turned it creaked like a rusty machine, and when he reached in his pocket for his handkerchief, the sounds of a minor avalanche filled the room. Even the beating of his heart (and the ticking of his watch) caused a commotion around him. The sound effects were hilariously psychotic, but they drew on deep sources of anxiety in the movie audience. The spectators were vicariously released from their own acute social embarrassment, in the kind of situation where one imagines something abysmal, like the dean farting at an important faculty meeting or a sudden belch escaping the lips of a grave personage. One immediately looks around uneasily to verify the truth of one's comic perceptions.

The physical presence of the body and its parts almost always arouses grotesque laughter, provided that the situation is relieved of its more immediate terrors. This may account for the massive presence of doctors in comic literature from the most ancient and disparate sources. Molière was particularly concerned with physicians as learned frauds, but the English Mummers' plays of folk literature always have a doctor on hand to resurrect the dead hero— and the plays are alarmingly specific about the fees demanded for this emergency service. Molière was also much preoccupied by invalids and hypochondriacs (as in *Le Malade Imaginaire*, 1673), who are all part of the same organic system. Our bodies are a source of humor because they are both trivial and vital, and we seem to perceive our physical processes and our illnesses as if we were outside ourselves. Again, the dualistic perspective encourages laughter. In Mann's *Magic Mountain*, Hans Castorp is so totally absorbed by the idea of illness that he solicits his beloved's tubercular X ray instead of a less expressive photograph.

Jokes on physical dismemberment (or its equivalent) have a long history, which turns on the shocking collocation of organic and inorganic parts. We need Bergson's theory again to remind us of our healthy, comic objections to the mechanization of life. The Boston Arm, invented at the Massachusetts Institute of Technology, gives us related visions of the Boston Strangler. Why do we react so strongly to prosthetic devices, so that the mere mention of a word like "merkin" (a pubic wig) can drive us into uncontrollable laughter? There is obviously an element of fear hidden in our response, and especially a symbolic fear of castration (or loss of parts). But beyond this gut reaction, there is also a sense of the body as a machine. The fruits of medical engineering question our vital humanity, and a person with a pacemaker, a glass eye, false teeth, a plastic knee cap, plates in his head, a Boston arm, glasses, a hearing aid, and a wig seems to attack our most cherished belief in organic integrity.

The old joke of the attractive woman disassembling herself in the privacy of her bedroom "After the Ball Was Over" turns on false appearances, but there is also a kind of fascinated horror at the body's standardized and easily replaceable equipment. It is curious that the upper-berth jokes recorded by Gershon Legman in his gargantuan anthology, *Rationale of the Dirty Joke*, all depend on mechanistic and voyeuristic assumptions of the body—always a female body—as a cunning device for sexual gratification. Upper-berth jokes, which have now virtually disappeared with the Pullman car and transcontinental trains (one of Legman's chief sources of material), are inherently simple, because there are only three worthwhile (and completely detachable) sexual parts. The gentleman in the upper berth—and he is always a gentleman and always in the upper berth—may well grow impatient at what he takes to be an excessive series of preliminary and superfluous detachments and unscrewings. One classic punch line is for the upper-berth gentleman to say petulantly: "Hey, lady, stop wasting time. You know what I want; just unscrew it and pass it up here." This is the archetypal comic situation of Bergson's essay on laughter, since it superimposes a mechanical conceit on the free-flowing and otherwise spontaneous nature of human experience.

Sexual jokes are particularly dependent on this shocking contrast, although there was an older, sporty gentleman in Laguna Beach, California, who always kept a glass eye handy, which he would suddenly slip into his mouth at appropriate moments to terrify and astound the children of the neighborhood. They could scarcely overcome their astonishment in time to laugh, even though they were allowed to handle the offending part, and, if lucky, to try it out. We laugh in order to master our metaphysical fear that our body is not unique—and may, in fact, have nothing whatsoever to do with our real self—and that our life force has somehow been mechanized and dehumanized. All of which reminds us inevitably of impotence, castration, and death, the three most important sources of anxious laughter.

The comic hero cultivates comic paranoia, as if laughter were an essential defense against a hostile reality.

Comic paranoia could be demonstrated biographically from the lives of the great comedians, or even from the lives of the second- and third-rate comics who figure in Phil Berger's *The Last Laugh: The World of the Stand-up Comic.* Woody Allen is in a long tradition of sad, neurotic, defensive clowns—schlemiels, nebbishes, mis- fits—whose wit is the only thing that keeps them going. These are the oppressed anti-heroes, beaten down by bureaucracy, baffled by the intricacies of the Machine Age, nonplussed by the mysteries of women and sex, who find it difficult to perform the simplest acts, but who nevertheless have feverish fantasies of their suppressed heroic potential, as Woody Allen recreates machismo roles in the style of Humphrey Bogart in *Play It Again Sam* (see Figure 19). There are similarly inflated dream sequences in most of Woody Allen's movies.

Admittedly, this is an extreme case, but comedians never seem to find reality warm, comforting, and supportive. Something is always going wrong, mistakes and accidents and unaccountable mishaps are at the heart of the typical intrigue plot in comedy, and the comic hero is usually trying to grapple with a highly resistant reality. He is always on his guard, always on the *qui vive*, always alert to disaster and instant chaos. Wit is a weapon with which to protect yourself, perhaps the only weapon. The sad clown is nei- ther powerful, rich, well-born, handsome, well-connected, or in any way favored by the gods. He must make his way alone, against overwhelming odds, with ridiculously inadequate equipment.

In a typically comic situation of this sort, not only is there a gross mismatch between the comic hero and the gigantic forces he is pitted against, but the comic hero is protected, as it were, by his own imperfect perception, or what may be called either innocence or stupidity. Mr. Magoo's extreme nearsightedness allows him to go through harrowing adventures with only the dimmest awareness of what is happening. He is constantly mumbling the platitudes of mistaken politeness in entirely inappropriate situations, and his hearty appeals to "Dear old Rutgers" usually come at moments of impending doom. Or the comic hero performs some heroic act unintentionally, striving for an effect just the opposite from what actually occurs. W. C. Fields inadvertently captures the robber in the *Bank Dick*, as does Inspector Clouseau (played by Peter Sellers) in *The Return of the Pink Panther*. The capture is an accidental by-product of something entirely different, but the comic anti-hero quickly adapts to his new status, since comic reality is inherently unstable, unsolid, unsubstantial, with an unlimited tendency to become unstuck. In these sudden transformations the element of surprise is negligible—Chaplin can become the Great Dictator and be changed back to the little tramp without violating our expectations. Comic reality is infinitely flexible, and heroic and unheroic roles are so easily interchangeable because the heroic and the grandiose are only illusions.

The point of these examples is that the comic hero is not at all daunted when reality turns against him, when chaos suddenly erupts, when madness takes over. His firm assumption is: *A Mad World, My Masters*, as in the title of the Jacobean comedy by Middleton (1606), or *It's a Mad Mad Mad Mad World* (1963), as in the title of the movie produced and directed by Stanley Kramer. The comic hero always sees reality as threatening, unpredictable, and explosive, and the appearance of placidity, amiability, calm, and domestic bliss is, of course, wildly misleading. The refrigerator purring so reassuringly is about to blow up, the family dog sleeping so effortlessly on the rug is about to go berserk and bite baby, and mother, putting her apple pie out to cool, will suddenly tear off her clothes and dance naked on the porch. Nothing can be taken for granted; the readiness is all.

The kind of comedian we are talking about never consciously tries to be funny. He doesn't laugh at his own jokes, and he certainly could not be called happy or joyous. He is, in fact, solemn, fearful, and glum, convinced that ultimate disaster is only moments away. Meanwhile, he devises hare-brained schemes that will prolong life for an instant or two longer. It is all futile, but comic ingenuity helps to pass the time. There is a firm conviction that he is the one sane man who remains alive in an otherwise distorted

Figure 19. Comic Machismo: Woody Allen as a Fantasy Pizza-Maker in *Play It Again Sam* (Paramount, 1972); *The Museum of Modern Art / Film Stills Archive.*

and surrealistic world. Again, "realism" proves to be a totally inadequate criterion for comedy. It is the grotesque twisting of the familiar that is the source of comedy, which cultivates a mood of blurred, out-of-focus perception, in which we have lost our clear vision, firm footing, and sense of rightness and decency. Comic paranoia suggests a certain fixed attitude to reality from which a good deal of comedy springs, although "paranoia" is perhaps too strong a term. It is evident, however, that comedy does not arise

Figure 20. A Battered W. C. Fields, with a Cunning Smile, Offers His Wife (Kathleen Howard) a Little Nosegay (*The Man on the Flying Trapeze*, Paramount, 1935); *The Museum of Modern Art / Film Stills Archive.*

from well-adjusted, middle-class persons, decent, hard-working, sane, with what psychiatrists call realistic goals and expectations. Comedy is produced rather from hysteria and frenzy and offers a technique for survival in a mad world.

If we separate respectable, upstanding citizens from the anarchic, irresponsible, and hostile world of comedy, we find not just two opposing views of reality, but rather two warring camps. W. C. Fields made a special point of shocking bourgeois sensibilities and the hoary shibboleths of home, love, family, and honor. In Figure 20, his offer of a small nosegay as a token of reconciliation to his fuming (but exceptionally well-marcelled) wife is patently fraudulent and cynical. "No man who hates dogs and children can be all bad" is one of his best-known apothegms, and his attempts to do grievous bodily harm to Baby Leroy are justly celebrated. His suggestion for his tombstone—"I'd rather be here than in Philadelphia"—is meant to shatter the dull propriety of that city.

Fields goes down in history as a strong dissenter against the Puritan ethic of Work and Purpose, as a creative drunkard, swindler, con man, and unenthusiastic husband and father. The facts of his life seem to support his image on the screen as a mistrustful, egotistic, ungenerous, and even paranoid man. But what a grandeur of gesture and language: a man always ready to reply, who almost persuades us that his vision of reality is richer and more appealing than our own narrow decency. Fields's acerbic wit has enormous attraction as a perfected and aesthetic lifestyle, and the sheer splendor of it makes us willing to suspend our moral disapproval and metaphysical disbelief. In the still from *You Can't Cheat an Honest Man*, which serves as frontispiece to this book, we see Fields in all of his comic splendor: beautifully decked out in a Western outfit, with frilled shirt, fringed leather pants, scruffy curled wig, and quizzical air.

This is an appropriate place to raise the nagging question whether comedy is cruel. It is certainly antisocial, if by society we mean to indicate the prevailing values. Comedy is almost by its very nature destructive and anarchic, and the comic hero tries to make his hesitant way outside the norms of society. He may have a new, mad vision that society must listen to in order to survive, but he is still an outcast and a pariah. Comedy is cruel because it takes a position apart from morality and accepted standards. The comic hero feels threatened by these criteria, and he doesn't agree to play by the rules. In an effort to survive, he engages in relentless guerrilla warfare with society.

Writers on satire insist on the moral corrective satire administers to an imperfect society, but in the kind of comedy we have been talking about, morality is definitely a middle-class luxury. Without his own stake in society, the buffoon cannot be expected to assent to the conservative ideals of satire. Satiric ridicule is a comfortable attitude. Comic heroes tend to fight dirty (if they fight at all), use foul language to stir people up (as Lenny Bruce did), and, considering the difficulty in merely staying alive, they generally ignore abstract questions of moral truth. Of course comedy is cruel—it may have to be cruel in order to exist, but cruelty is mitigated by wit, and the whole performance is imaginative and dreamlike and removed from the contested arena of ethical debate.

The comic hero may serve as the ritual clown of his society, acting as a scapegoat for its taboos.

The theory and practice of the ritual clown is well documented from the study of various Indian tribes of the Southwest, especially the Zuñi Katcinas. The annual appointment of a ritual clown provides an ingenious safety valve for the pressures, guilts, and accumulated repressions of the society. Like the scapegoat, the clown takes upon himself all the taboos of the society and spends his time obscenely flouting everything decent and sacred. He masturbates publicly, covers himself with excrement, makes sexual advances to virgins and married women alike, utters forbidden words, and openly blasphemes against the gods. His outrageous conduct fills his auditors with emotions of loathing, fear, and terror, since they expect the gods to strike him down at any moment. But the clown plays his carefully assigned role with merriment and abandon. He is a jester, a sacred fool, who has license to break all taboos during the time he is on stage. It is all very histrionic, and the ritual clowning functions like an extended theatrical performance, in which the audience, through catharsis, is released vicariously from its burdensome fears and taboos. The ritual clown acts out a forbidden social role for the general good of the community.

This institutionalized clowning has many analogies in more advanced societies. Mardi Gras, the last day before Lent, develops from church ritual, and it offers a period of wild merrymaking, colorful pageantry, and general license. The medieval church provided various forms of ritual release, including the ceremonies connected with the Boy Bishop, in which all accepted forms and formalities were reversed, and the boy helpers in the church took over the august offices. This kind of occasion gave the opportunity for all sorts of mockery, parody, and even blasphemy, but within a framework of official tolerance. The official sanction marks the distinction between mere clowning and ritual clowning, which only occurs within prescribed limits and for a brief duration. It is holiday contrasted with everyday.

The fool in Shakespeare functions against a background of real fools, who were part of noble households in the Elizabethan period, either natural fools crazed in their wits or professional jesters, or some combination of the two. The fool in *King Lear* doesn't have the sophistication of such professionals as Touchstone in *As You Like It* and Feste in *Twelfth Night*, and his acerbic, eccentric manner seems closer to genuine madness, as Melville certainly thought in his recreation of the fool as Pip in *Moby-Dick*. At a critical point in the play, Lear can only speak to the fool and Poor Tom, the Bedlam beggar (Edgar in disguise). The fool understands Lear's folly as no one else can, and he speaks by allowance and permission. In a sense, he is totally fearless, despite Lear's continual references to the whip, by which the fool could be officially chastized. The fool becomes the ritual scapegoat for everything that is troubling the old king, but he is also a philosopher and moral instructor as well. Since he is completely outside the social hierarchy, he is free to speak and to act without constraint; it is as if, except for his role as ritual clown, he had no separate being at all. He exists for the sake of King Lear: to mitigate his passion and to offer him an elemental commiseration and comfort, and also, in another sense, to be the lost son that Lear never had.

The fool and the ritual clown are far from any heroic notion of the comic hero, yet they fulfill a necessary and vital function. They are the most humble of creatures, the lowest on the social scale, completely anonymous and insignificant. Yet as truth-speakers they are endowed with a terrifying power. They are not, of course, aware that they are anything so exalted as truth-speakers. They merely act their role according to the prescribed forms and in an unsophisticated and unselfconscious way. Their purposeful folly and licensed wit free them from the restraints of ordinary men, and witnesses have testified to the ambiguous mixture of grossness, stupidity, and awesomeness in the ritual clown. The assumption is that the gods speak through their appointed fool, who is a mouthpiece for their dark and inscrutable wisdom, and who may actually be privy to their secrets. The ritual aspect overrides any personal considerations, and we arrive at the central concept of the sacred fool, who is the gods' minion. In this hypothesis, the gods are not orderly and predictable, but vast, chaotic, incomprehensible, and even obscene forces. Ritual clowning and the role of the fool offer a way of mastering a mysterious and anarchic reality.

In his essays on joking relationships, Radcliffe-Brown has studied how ritual clowning also provides a safety valve for ordinary social dealings that might arouse hostility. In the highly formalized joking relationship between two persons, "one is by custom permitted, and in some instances required, to tease or make fun of the other, who in turn is required to take no offence." The fixed and histrionic social roles neutralize anticipated aggressions and ritualize and formalize "permitted disrespect." Thus, among the Dogon in Africa, a man stands in a joking relationship to his wife's sisters and their daughters. In our society, a married man might have a joking relationship with his mother-in-law, a highly traditional source of jokes. The hostility is both expressed and contained at the same time, and the rituals of social life smooth over personal difficulties. By acting the role of ritual clown, the son-in-law manages to depersonalize his volatile role.

The comic hero doesn't eventually merge into the tragic hero, but represents an entirely different range of experience.

It is unfashionable, and perhaps even unsporting, to insist that comedy is separate from tragedy and to resist the proposition that all comedy aspires to the condition of tragedy. We must reject the glib assumption that comedy is a lesser form of art and experience that somehow needs to be ennobled and completed by tragedy. Dramatic criticism usually hunts out ways in which comedy may lay claim to darker overtones and a tragic coloring. Shakespeare's "problem" comedies—*Measure for Measure, Troilus and Cressida, All's*

Well That Ends Well—are conventionally praised for the wrong reasons, and their supposed resemblance to tragedy immediately elevates their status in the Shakespearean canon. Jonson's *Volpone* has been similarly extolled for its tragic implications, while its comic brilliance is awkwardly acknowledged but minimized. Thus Molière's vigorous and uncompromising comedy, *Le Misanthrope*, is distorted by the tragic perspective, and more recent playwrights like Beckett, Pinter, and Dürrenmatt may suffer from our inability to appreciate comedy—even dark comedy, tragicomedy, tragic farce, or whatever we may choose to call it—without putting in facile claims for the "seriousness" of tragedy.

It may be useful to remind readers that comedy has always been the dominant dramatic form. Shakespeare wrote almost twice as many comedies as tragedies, and the tragedies and histories are permeated with comic materials. The reverse is not true, and although the comedies may have moving and pathetic scenes, they are not in any way permeated with tragic materials. And in the whole corpus of Elizabethan drama tragedy is rather uncommon. If we insist on tragedies after the model of Aristotle's *Poetics*, then true Elizabethan tragedy is extremely rare, and most of Shakespeare's tragedies do not qualify. The point must be that it is extremely difficult to write tragedy, since the form itself depends upon moral and metaphysical assumptions. Tragedy as we know it apparently doesn't exist in certain oriental cultures, whereas comedy is much more universal and isn't so strongly affected by cultural differences. One hears it categorically stated nowadays that tragedy is dead, and that comedy has absorbed the techniques and potentialities of tragedy. This is not the sort of assertion that we can demonstrate to be either true or false, but it is certainly difficult to write tragedy in a period when the theological superstructure has been removed, as Arthur Miller has discovered to his peril. He has tried in a number of plays to refashion the basic tragic formulas of *Death of a Salesman* with ever-diminishing effect. He has now apparently abandoned the writing of tragedy.

This is not intended to attack tragedy and the possibilities of true tragedy in our time, but only to insist on some of the differences between comedy and tragedy. Traditionally, tragedy ends in death (or its equivalent, like the blinding of Oedipus), whereas comedy ends in marriage, feasting, dancing, the promise of babies, and a general mood of reconciliation. Death, or the threat of death, is always unreal in comedy, and even more unreal in tragicomedy, where it is only an effect of manipulation. Once death is removed as a possibility, the system of serious punishments and rewards breaks down, and we have to rely on poetic justice. Comedy doesn't allow for grave punishments at all, but it moves towards untangling complications and reconciling enemies. The expected happy ending of comedy still makes a great deal of difference in the kind of causes needed to produce the programmed result.

In Horace Walpole's famous dictum, "The world is a comedy to those that think, a tragedy to those that feel." In other words, human involvement produces tragedy, while the comic hero remains aloof from the events in which he participates. He doesn't feel deeply. In the sense of sympathy and commiseration, he probably doesn't feel at all. The tragic hero is committed, a man of principle, profoundly flawed or mistaken, but still serious, moral, open to the effects of choice and free will, and ready to take the moral consequences of his acts. None of these noble qualities applies to the comic hero, except fortuitously. He engages in adventures and encounters in which chance plays a large role, but he never truly feels sorrow, guilt, compassion, or any of the legitimately tragic emotions.

In the classic example, if we see someone trip on a banana peel we laugh, especially if it is a well-dressed and self-important person. But if we become aware that the person has broken his arm (or is otherwise seriously injured), we stop laughing. The wound draws our human pity and neutralizes laughter. In the dynamics of sick humor, however, we laugh when we see the person slip, but laugh even harder when we learn that he has broken his arm. We refuse our sympathy and insist on the full measure of retribution for persons who deserve (and need) our corrective laughter. But even sick humor would draw the line at persons whom we know and love. It is impossible to laugh at the injury of those near and dear to us, except in a condition of uncontrolled hysteria. It is this line of feeling that completely separates tragedy and comedy.

In the typically sick joke, there is an outrageously cruel and insensitive statement, as in the slogan: "Hire the Handicapped;

They're Fun to Watch," or the Helen Keller title: "Around the Block in Eighty Days." We don't mean to make fun of handicapped persons in general or Helen Keller in particular, but we delight in our comic impudence. There is, in fact, a whole collection of Helen Keller jokes on the model of: "Did you hear the one about the man who gave Helen Keller a hot waffle iron to read, and she thought it was braille?" We can only laugh by abstracting painful or embarrassing situations and insulating ourselves, momentarily at least, from all human feelings. Sick humor provides its own special catharsis for the violation of taboos, and it offers an interesting test case of the distinction between comedy and tragedy. When we tell a sick joke, we are deliberately pushing the alienation of human sympathies, that comedy demands, to an absurd, outer limit. We can only laugh by choosing to ignore the obvious human content that would make the joke tragic.

There still remains a serious theoretical question whether comedy is the obverse of tragedy, with both together defining the whole range of human experience. This dualistic formula sounds comforting, but in practice comedy and tragedy widely overlap. Comedy is not composed of the things tragedy is not—its leftovers, as it were, nor is it a lower form or trivialization of tragedy. These formulations are objectionable because comedy is a different kind of experience from tragedy, and it may well be that, although comedy has innumerable resemblances to tragedy (and also direct contrasts with it), the one form has no essential relation to the other. This statement violates a humanistic assumption about the organic connection of literary forms and genres, but comedy has been so glibly subordinated to tragedy that it becomes important to insist that comedy and tragedy are different entities in their own right.

Comic catharsis is often equated with catharsis in tragedy, and Aristotle's *Poetics*, which formulates the idea of the purging of pity and fear, was cleverly reversed in antiquity to produce his unwritten (or lost) treatise on comedy (as reconstructed in Lane Cooper's *An Aristotelian Theory of Comedy*). The procedure seems highly irregular, since no justification is offered for the belief that tragedy and comedy are analogous systems. Whatever we may think about that question, we may still ask: Is there a comic equivalent for tragic catharsis? Comedy, too, arouses strong and even violent emotions, but the relief and mollification that comedy finally brings seem to lie in the area of beneficial wish fulfillment. We are allowed to work through our anxieties about our limited capacities and powers. Gut laughter provides for the release of primitive drives and instinctual needs that may be suppressed in daily life. It is a ritual release shared with other members of the audience. We are engaged in vicarious play, sometimes with great intensity. Comic catharsis purges inhibitions and obstructions alike and lets us express a grandiose, heroic, and eloquent vision of ourselves—a vision that gains force from being so demonstrably untrue.

Notes
on Sources,
with Suggestions
for Further Reading

Of the many general introductions to comedy, I will only mention a few that I found informative and well written. Max Eastman's *Enjoyment of Laughter* (New York: Simon & Schuster, 1936) is still an enjoyable collection of jokes and stories, especially American, interspersed with sensible comments on the art of comedy. Eastman's earlier book, *The Sense of Humor* (New York: Scribner, 1922) is a genial discussion of theories of humor. In *The Hyacinth Room* (New York: Knopf, 1964), Cyrus Hoy considers types of comedy, tragedy, and tragicomedy, with full attention to defining his ideas

179

through dramatic examples. John Palmer's elegant little book, *Comedy* (London: Secker, 1914), is valuable for its awareness of the social context. Among recent academic books sensitive to popular comedy, we may single out Elmer M. Blistein, *Comedy in Action* (Durham, N.C.: Duke University Press, 1964), and Morton Gurewitch, *Comedy: The Irrational Vision* (Ithaca, N.Y.: Cornell University Press, 1975).

The best collection of essays on comedy is by Robert W. Corrigan, *Comedy: Meaning and Form* (San Francisco: Chandler, 1965), a generous book of 481 pages. Paul Lauter's *Theories of Comedy* (Garden City, N.Y.: Doubleday, Anchor Press, 1964) is more historical than Corrigan's, but the selections are too short. An authoritative collection of literary essays on comedy is by W. K. Wimsatt, *The Idea of Comedy: Ben Jonson to George Meredith* (Englewood Cliffs, N.J.: Prentice Hall, 1969). Harry Levin gathers an attractive group of critical essays in *Veins of Humor* (Cambridge, Mass.: Harvard University Press, 1972). The first issue of *New York Literary Forum* (1978), "Comedy: New Perspectives," edited by Maurice Charney, brings together seventeen essays on various aspects of comedy and a translation of Feydeau's last play, *Hortense a dit: "Je m'en fous."*

The only separate bibliography is E. H. Mikhail's very inadequate volume, with 320 entries to the end of 1970: *Comedy and Tragedy: A Bibliography of Critical Studies* (Troy, N.Y.: Whitston, 1972). The specialized studies of comedy by psychologists and psychoanalysts are listed in detail in the fifteen-page bibliography by Jeffrey H. Goldstein and Paul E. McGhee included in their collection of essays, *The Psychology of Humor: Theoretical Perspectives and Empirical Issues* (New York: Academic Press, 1972). This covers the period from 1900 to August 1971. There is also a good review of the psychological literature in J. C. Flugel, "Humor and Laughter," in Gardner Lindzey, ed., *Handbook of Social Psychology* (Cambridge, Mass.: Addison-Wesley, 1954), Vol. II, 709–34.

Preface

For the major books on which my study is based (p. xii), Henri Bergson's treatise, *Laughter* (1900), is conveniently available in a paperback called *Comedy*, edited by Wylie Sypher, who contributes a long essay on "The Meanings of Comedy" (Garden City, N.Y.: Doubleday, Anchor Press, 1956). Sigmund Freud's *Jokes and Their Relation to the Unconscious* (1905), translated by James Strachey, is in the series of Freud's shorter works (New York: Norton, 1960). Strachey's translation is much superior to that of A. A. Brill in *The Basic Writings of Sigmund Freud* (New York: Modern Library, 1938). Freud's later essay, "Humour," modifies some of his earlier ideas and may be found in *Collected Papers*, Volume V, ed. James Strachey (London: Hogarth Press, 1928), 215–21.

Northrop Frye's stimulating ideas about comedy, especially New Comedy, are most fully expressed in *Anatomy of Criticism* (Princeton: Princeton University Press, 1957), pp. 163–86, which expands a discussion first presented as "The Argument of Comedy," *English Institute Essays 1948* (New York: Columbia University Press, 1949). Frye is strongly influenced by the ritualistic theories of Francis M. Cornford in *The Origin of Attic Comedy* (Cambridge: Cambridge University Press, 1934). Cedric Whitman has an excellent discussion of Aristophanes and the assumptions of Old Comedy in *Aristophanes and the Comic Hero* (Cambridge, Mass.: Harvard University Press, 1964); Whitman is skeptical about the *alazon* (imposter) / *eiron* (sly man) theories of Cornford and Frye.

Festive comedy has its roots in popular festivals and social customs that are teasingly related to literature. For the Shakespearean background, see C. L. Barber's important book, *Shakespeare's Festive Comedy: A Study of Dramatic Form and its Relation to Social Custom* (Princeton: Princeton University Press, 1959). Mikhail Bakhtin has a very extensive study of Rabelais emphasizing carnival and an intense self-consciousness of the body and its functions: *Rabelais and His World*, tr. Helene Iswolsky (Cambridge, Mass.: Massachusetts Institute of Technology Press, 1968). Unfortunately, the translation is crude and almost unreadable. I should also mention the elaborate literature on fools, especially Enid Welsford's delightful book, *The Fool* (Garden City, N.Y.: Doubleday, Anchor Press, 1961). Also recommended are: Barbara Swain, *Fools and Folly during the Middle Ages and the Renaissance* (New York: Columbia University Press, 1932) and William Willeford, *The Fool and His Scepter: A Study in Clowns and Jesters and Their Audience* (Evanston, Ill.: Northwestern University Press, 1969).

There is more writing on comedy, humor, and related topics

such as tickling by psychologists than by any other intellectual group. Some of this literature is highly technical and belongs rather in the area of physiology and medical research, as, for example, the short book of Frederic R. Stearns, *Laughing: Physiology, Pathophysiology, Psychology, Pathopsychology and Development* (Springfield, Ill.: Charles C. Thomas, 1972). Charles Darwin's study of the physiology of comic expression in Chapter 8 of *The Expression of the Emotions in Man and Animals* (London: Murray, 1904) is still authoritative. Two fascinating journal articles in this area are: Ernest L. Lloyd, "The Respiratory Mechanism in Laughter," *Journal of General Psychology*, XIX (1938), 179–89, and Endre Petö, "Weeping and Laughing," *International Journal of Psychoanalysis*, XXVII (1946), 129–33.

Some of the older psychological books are excellent introductions to laughter and comedy, especially in their skillful summary of various theories. I would particularly recommend J. C. Gregory, *The Nature of Laughter* (London: Kegan Paul, 1924), which is very lucid. Also valuable are: J. Y. T. Greig, *The Psychology of Laughter and Comedy* (New York: Dodd Mead, 1923), and Ralph Piddington, *The Psychology of Laughter: A Study in Social Adaptation* (New York: Gamut Press, 1963). The newer psychological literature is well represented in the collection of Jeffrey H. Goldstein and Paul E. McGhee, *The Psychology of Humor: Theoretical Perspectives and Empirical Issues* (New York: Academic Press, 1972), and in Jacob Levine, *Motivation in Humor* (New York: Atherton Press, 1969). A good example of the psychological approach to humor is the important article by Frederick C. Redlich, Jacob Levine, and Theodore P. Sohler, "A Mirth Response Test: Preliminary Report on a Psychodiagnostic Technique Utilizing Dynamics of Humor," *American Journal of Orthopsychiatry*, XXI (1951), 717–34.

The psychoanalytic approach to comedy is strongly dependent on Freud. Martin Grotjahn's *Beyond Laughter* (New York: McGraw-Hill, 1957) makes a good introduction to the subject. Ernst Kris, *Psychoanalytic Explorations in Art* (New York: Schocken, 1964) is much more complex. Developing material only sketched in Freud, Martha Wolfenstein has written a warm and stimulating book called *Children's Humor: A Psychological Analysis* (Glencoe, Ill.: Free Press, 1954). Ludwig Eidelberg's analysis of a joke by Mae West is a minor classic of humor in its own right: "A Contribution to the Study of Wit," *Psychoanalytic Review*, XXXII (1945), 33–61.

Eric Bentley's account of farce (p. xiii) began as an essay, "The Psychology of Farce," which introduces his collection of farces, *Let's Get a Divorce! and Other Plays* (New York: Hill & Wang, 1958). This essay is expanded but not necessarily improved in Bentley's book, *The Life of the Drama* (New York: Atheneum, 1964).

I. The language and rhetoric of comedy

Joe Miller's Jests: or, The Wits Vade-Mecum (1739), cited on p. 10, is a classic collection of amusing anecdotes and traditional stories. Many of these brief, numbered items are not jokes at all in our more restricted sense of the term. Dover Books offers a facsimile reprint of the original edition (New York, 1963).

Cornford and Frye's contribution to the discussion of irony (pp. 10–11) is noted in the previous section. For further reading on irony, I would suggest two original and stimulating books: G. G. Sedgewick, *Of Irony, Especially in Drama* (Toronto: University of Toronto Press, 1934) and Alan Reynolds Thompson, *The Dry Mock: A Study of Irony in Drama* (Berkeley: University of California Press, 1948). Both interpret irony broadly and make a valuable contribution to our understanding of comedy.

The Eisenhower examples (pp. 13 and 15) are quoted from Dwight Macdonald, *Parodies: An Anthology from Chaucer to Beerbohm—and After* (New York: Random House, 1965). See also the *Parody Anthology* by Carolyn Wells (New York: Dover, 1967), which is entirely in verse.

Caricature (pp. 14 and 15) is ably discussed and illustrated in Ernst Kris, *Psychoanalytic Explorations in Art* (New York: Schocken, 1964); Section 7, "The Principles of Caricature," is written in collaboration with the art historian, E. H. Gombrich. Many of the critical terms on pp. 15 and 18 are more fully defined, especially in their relation to poetry, in the *Encyclopedia of Poetry and Poetics*, ed. Alex Preminger (Princeton: Princeton University Press, 1965).

Kitsch and camp (pp. 16–18) have been widely studied and illustrated, particularly in books on painting and the industrial arts, with a strong emphasis on works of middle-European origin. Gillo Dorfles has edited *Kitsch: The World of Bad Taste* (New York: Universe Books, 1969), which is a grab bag of pictures and text of widely varying merit and interest. The section on "pornokitsch" is the most attractive. For camp we are fortunate to have Susan Sontag's incisive essay, "Notes on 'Camp'," in *Against Interpretation* (New York: Dell, 1966), pp. 275–92.

Darwin A. Hindman's *1800 Riddles, Enigmas and Conundrums* (New York: Dover, 1963), from which I draw many examples on p. 21 and elsewhere, is the best collection of an old-fashioned, question-and-answer type of humor. Antony B. Lake's anthology, *A Pleasury of Witticisms and Word Play* (New York: Hart, 1975), is not as startling as Hindman's.

Terry Southern and Mason Hoffenberg's novel, *Candy* (New York: Putnam, 1964), quoted on pp. 28–29, is worth studying not only for its parody of Voltaire's *Candide*, but also for its deft ridicule of the bland optimism of the Eisenhower era and the kind of literature published in the slick magazines of that period. Ionesco's play, *The Bald Soprano* (pp. 30 and 32–34), is quoted from Donald M. Allen's translation in Eugène Ionesco, *Four Plays* (New York: Grove Press, 1958). Ionesco's opinions about Caragiale (p. 29) are quoted from his *Notes and Counter Notes*, tr. Donald Watson (New York: Grove Press, 1964), which is a valuable collection of the playwright's comments on the art of comedy.

Boners (pp. 35–36) are conveniently gathered in *The Pocket Book of Boners: An Omnibus of Schoolboy Howlers and Unconscious Humor* (New York: Pocket Books, 1941).

Martial (p. 41) is quoted from Rolfe Humphries' lively versions in *Martial: Selected Epigrams* (Bloomington: Indiana University Press, 1963), and Herrick (p. 42) from *The Poetical Works of Robert Herrick*, ed. L. C. Martin (Oxford: Clarendon Press, 1956). For further discussion see Hoyt Hopewell Hudson, *The Epigram in the English Renaissance* (Princeton: Princeton University Press, 1947).

For limericks (pp. 43–44), Louis Untermeyer has a pleasant selection in *Lots of Limericks: Light, Lusty, and Lasting* (New York: Bell, 1961), but Gershon Legman's *The Limerick* (New York: Bell, 1969), consisting of 1700 items all erotic, with notes and variants, is a much more impressive group. A second large volume entitled *The New Limerick* was published by Crown in 1977.

II. Comic characters: Conventions and types

The origins and early history of the *commedia dell' arte* (p. 55) are traced in Allardyce Nicoll, *Masks, Mimes, and Miracles* (New York: Harcourt, Brace, 1931). See also Pierre Louis Duchartre, *The Italian Comedy*, tr. Randolph T. Weaver (New York: Dover, 1966). Both books are profusely illustrated.

Plautus (p. 63 and elsewhere) is quoted from Lionel Casson's translations into musical-comedy Americanese. What used to be *Six Plays of Plautus*, published by Doubleday, Anchor Press, has now been divided by Norton into *Amphitryon & Two Other Plays* and *The Menaechmus Twins & Two Other Plays* (New York, 1971). Readers may pursue their interest in Plautus in Erich Segal's introductory book, *Roman Laughter: The Comedy of Plautus* (Cambridge, Mass.: Harvard University Press, 1968); in George Duckworth, *The Nature of Roman Comedy: A Study in Popular Entertainment* (Princeton: Princeton University Press, 1952), which puts a valuable emphasis on staging; and in Alan McN. G. Little's impressive article, "Plautus and Popular Drama," *Harvard Studies in Classical Philology*, XLIX (1938), 205–28.

The comic art of Ben Jonson (pp. 63–64 and elsewhere) may profitably be studied in Jonas A. Barish, *Ben Jonson and the Language of Prose Comedy* (New York: Norton, 1970) and in John J. Enck, *Jonson and the Comic Truth* (Madison: University of Wisconsin Press, 1966). Jonson's works are quoted from the Yale Ben Jonson, whose general editors are Alvin B. Kernan and Richard B. Young. *Bartholomew Fair* is edited by Eugene M. Waith (New Haven: Yale University Press, 1963) and *The Alchemist* by Alvin B. Kernan (New Haven: Yale University Press, 1974).

There are a great many resources for understanding Shakespeare's comedy (pp. 64–65 and elsewhere), but none more impressive than Leo Salingar's *Shakespeare and the Traditions of Comedy*, which has just appeared in a paperback edition (Cambridge: Cambridge University Press, 1976). This is valuable for its study of the classical backgrounds of comedy, as well as those of the Middle Ages and the Italian Renaissance. We have already mentioned C. L. Barber's stimulating book, *Shakespeare's Festive Comedy* (Princeton: Princeton University Press, 1959), to which we should add Ralph Berry's provocative *Shakespeare's Comedies: Explorations in Form* (Princeton: Princeton University Press, 1972). Shakespeare is quoted throughout from the paperback volumes in the Signet Classic Shakespeare, edited by Sylvan Barnet and published by New American Library. The comic drama of Shakespeare's time is well represented in Brian Gibbons, *Jacobean City Comedy: A Study of Satiric Plays by Jonson, Marston and Middleton* (Cambridge, Mass.: Harvard University Press, 1968) and in Alexander Leggatt, *Citizen Comedy in the Age of Shakespeare* (Toronto: University of Toronto Press, 1973).

Machiavelli's *Mandragola* (p. 67 and elsewhere) is quoted from the translation by Anne and Henry Paolucci in the Library of Liberal Arts (Indianapolis, Ind.: Bobbs-Merrill, n.d.). I have translated Molière (pp. 67–68 and elsewhere) myself to make a certain point about the satirical effect, but I don't pretend to compete with Richard Wilbur's superb verse translations: *Tartuffe* (New York: Harcourt, Brace & World, 1963), *The Misanthrope* (New York: Harcourt, Brace & World, 1965), and *The School for Wives* (New York: Harcourt Brace Jovanovich, 1971).

III. The structure of comedy

On the general subject of dramatic structure, see Jackson Barry's lucid book, *Dramatic Structure: The Shaping of Experience* (Berkeley: University of California Press, 1970). Richard Levin demonstrates a method of dealing with structure, both tragic and comic, in *The Multiple Plot in English Renaissance Drama* (Chicago: University of Chicago Press, 1971). Structure in the large, mythic sense is an important theme in Northrop Frye's *Anatomy of Criticism* (Princeton: Princeton University Press, 1957) and in Susanne K. Langer's *Feeling and Form* (New York: Scribner, 1953), especially in her wide-ranging Chapter 18: "The Great Dramatic Forms: The Comic Rhythm."

For Georges Feydeau (pp. 87–88 and elsewhere), I recommend the brilliant translations by Norman R. Shapiro in *Four Farces by Georges Feydeau* (Chicago: University of Chicago Press, 1970) and in the comedy issue of *New York Literary Forum*. Shapiro fully translates Feydeau's comic idiom into American equivalents.

An Essay on Comedy by George Meredith (p. 90), first published in 1877, is conveniently available in *Comedy*, edited by Wylie Sypher (Garden City, N.Y.: Doubleday, Anchor Press, 1956). As a theoretical statement on comedy, this essay is disappointing, although it does make some good points about the essential role of women.

IV. Forms of comedy: Farce, tragic farce, burlesque, comedy of manners, satire, and festive comedy

Eric Bentley's essay, "The Psychology of Farce," mentioned above (p. 183), is one of the best accounts of the genre. In a revised form, the essay appears as part of Bentley's book, *The Life of the Drama* (New York: Atheneum, 1964). It is reprinted in Robert W. Corrigan's excellent anthology, *Comedy: Meaning and Form* (San Francisco: Chandler, 1965), with two other pieces on farce by Vsevolod Meyerhold and Robert C. Stephenson.

The assumptions of tragic farce are brilliantly laid out in Mathew Winston's essay, "*Humour noir* and Black Humor," in *Veins of Humor*, ed. Harry Levin (Cambridge, Mass.: Harvard University Press, 1972), pp. 269–84 and in a companion essay "Black Humor: To Weep with Laughing" in *New York Literary Forum*, Vol. I. T. S. Eliot's piece on Marlowe (pp. 106–7) appears in his *Selected Essays 1917–1932* (New York: Harcourt Brace, 1932) and in his *Essays on Elizabethan Drama* (New York: Harcourt, Brace & World, 1956). Friedrich Dürrenmatt's essay, "Problems of the Theatre" (p. 107), is published by Grove Press with *The Marriage of Mr. Mississippi* in a translation by Gerhard Nellhaus (New York, n.d.). A general account of Beckett, Pinter, Ionesco, and other contemporary playwrights may be found in Martin Esslin, *The Theatre of the Absurd* (Garden City, N.Y.: Doubleday, Anchor Press, 1961). All the plays discussed in this section appear in editions published by Grove Press, New York.

The burlesque plays are mostly quoted from the excellent anthology by Simon Trussler, *Burlesque Plays of the Eighteenth Century* (London: Oxford University Press, 1969). Barron's Educational Series prints Buckingham's *The Rehearsal* and Sheridan's *The Critic* in a single paperback volume (Great Neck, N.Y., 1960).

An excellent introduction to the spirit of comedy of manners is John Palmer, *The Comedy of Manners* (New York: Russell & Russell, 1962). Among the many books on Restoration comedy, we may single out Thomas H. Fujimura, *The Restoration Comedy of Wit* (Princeton: Princeton University Press, 1952); Kathleen M. Lynch, *The Social Mode of Restoration Comedy* (New York: Octagon Books, 1965); and Bonamy Dobrée, *Restoration Comedy, 1660–1720* (London: Oxford University Press, 1966). See also Ian Donaldson, *The World Upside-Down: Comedy from Jonson to Fielding* (Oxford: Clarendon Press, 1970). Two valuable collections of essays on Restoration drama are by John Loftis (New York: Oxford University Press, 1966) and Earl Miner (Englewood Cliffs, N.J.: Prentice-Hall, 1966).

For the theory and practice of satire, a subject beyond the scope of this book, see David Worcester, *The Art of Satire* (Cambridge, Mass.: Harvard University Press, 1940), and Alvin Kernan, *The Cankered Muse* (New Haven: Yale University Press, 1959). Oscar James Campbell offers a vigorous and polemical account of the harsher side of satire in *Shakespeare's Satire* (Hamden, Conn.: Archon Books, 1963).

The art of Molière (pp. 130–34) is trenchantly evaluated in W. G. Moore's short book, *Molière: A New Criticism* (Oxford: Clarendon Press, 1969). See also Lionel Gossman, *Men and Masks: A Study of Molière* (Baltimore: Johns Hopkins Press, 1963), and Judd D. Hubert, *Molière and the Comedy of Intellect* (Berkeley: University of California Press, 1962). Bergson's essay, *Laughter*, draws largely on Molière for its examples (in *Comedy*, Garden City, N.Y.:

Doubleday, Anchor Press, 1956). For Shaw (pp. 134–35), Eric Bentley's *Bernard Shaw* (Norfolk, Conn.: New Directions, 1947) is enlightening.

For festive comedy, the books by Barber, Bakhtin, Whitman, and others have already been accounted for on p. 181.

V. Comedy in theory and in practice: Seven aspects of the comic hero

Among many possibilities, two stimulating books on the theory of comedy are Albert Cook, *The Dark Voyage and the Golden Mean* (Cambridge, Mass.: Harvard University Press, 1949), and Elder Olson, *The Theory of Comedy* (Bloomington, Ind.: Indiana University Press, 1968).

There are many good books on the films and film comedians mentioned in this section, including biographies and cinematographies. Walter Kerr's recent contribution, *The Silent Clowns* (New York: Knopf, 1975), is particularly attractive. For critical books, see Raymond Durgnat, *The Crazy Mirror: Hollywood Comedy and the American Image* (London: Faber & Faber, 1969); Gerald Mast, *The Comic Mind: Comedy and the Movies* (Indianapolis, Ind.: Bobbs-Merrill, 1973); and John Montgomery, *Comedy Films 1894–1954*, 2 ed. (London: Allen & Unwin, 1968). David Robinson has a very informative little book called *Buster Keaton* (Bloomington, Ind.: Indiana University Press, 1969).

The Freudian and psychological theories may be explored in the books and articles mentioned on pp. 181–83.

The play theories of Huizinga (pp. 155–57) are developed in his book, *Homo Ludens: A Study of the Play-Element in Culture* (Boston: Beacon Press, 1955), which challenges Freudian notions about play. The folk plays of the English Mummers (p. 165) have been collected by R. J. E. Tiddy in *The Mummers' Play* (Oxford: Clarendon Press, 1923). Gershon Legman's mammoth study of erotic folklore, *Rationale of the Dirty Joke: An Analysis of Sexual Humor*, First Series (New York: Grove Press, 1971) is completed by a second series of grosser and more violent jokes, *No Laughing Matter* (New

York: Bell, 1975). I refer to Legman on p. 166. Phil Berger's rambling book (p. 167), *The Last Laugh: The World of the Stand-Up Comics* (New York: Ballantine Books, 1975), gathers together odds and ends of biographical reminiscence and bits from gag writers' scripts.

There is a rich anthropological and sociological literature relevant to comedy (pp. 172–74), especially the studies of ritual clowning in various cultures, most notably the American Indian. Julian H. Steward analyzes the main lines of the topic very concisely in "The Ceremonial Buffoon of the American Indian," *Papers of the Michigan Academy of Science, Arts and Letters*, XIV (1930), 187–207. The subject is more fully detailed in Ruth L. Bunzel, "Zuñi Katcinas," Bureau of American Ethnology, Annual Report #47, 1929–30 (Washington, D.C., 1932), pp. 837–1108. See also Elsie Clews Parsons and Ralph L. Beals, "The Sacred Clowns of the Pueblo and Mayo-Yaqui Indians," *American Anthropologist*, N.S., XXXVI (1934), 491–514; and Lucile Hoerr Charles, "The Clown's Function," *Journal of American Folklore*, LVIII (1945), 25–34. There is a good essay by Jacob Levine, "Regression in Primitive Clowning," *Psychoanalytic Quarterly*, XXX (1961), 72–83, which is reprinted in his anthology, *Motivation in Humor* (New York: Atherton Press, 1969). A. R. Radcliffe-Brown has two important studies of joking relationships in *Structure and Function in Primitive Society* (New York: Free Press, 1965).

On the general relation of comedy to tragedy (pp. 174–78) see Walter Kerr, *Tragedy and Comedy* (New York: Simon & Schuster, 1967), which unfortunately subordinates comedy to tragedy. Lane Cooper's reconstruction of Aristotle's supposed treatise on comedy (p. 177) appears in his book, *An Aristotelian Theory of Comedy* (New York: Kraus, 1969). This is an ingenious, learned, but curiously hypothetical study.

Index

191